WISCONSIN
AT ANTIETAM

The Badger State's Sacrifice on America's Bloodiest Day

CAL SCHOONOVER

THE
History
PRESS

Published by The History Press
Charleston, SC
www.historypress.com

Cover images courtesy of the Library of Congress.

First published 2020

Manufactured in the United States

ISBN 9781467142151

Library of Congress Control Number: 2020930462

To the fighting men of the Iron Brigade and the sacrifices they made to keep all men free. Also, to my dad, Jim, who passed down his interest of history to me. We miss you dearly.

CONTENTS

ACKNOWLEDGEMENTS

No one takes on a major study of any kind without help; that applies to this volume as well. I began my interest in the Civil War in the 1980s, when my parents took my sisters and me to Washington, D.C. My late father, a Vietnam veteran, wanted to see the newly erected wall dedicated to the fallen soldiers who had given their all in Vietnam. It was during this trip that I remember seeing the large statue of Abraham Lincoln at the Lincoln Memorial. We also visited the graves of Civil War soldiers in Arlington National Cemetery. Those two experiences sparked my desire to know more about Civil War history.

Since that time, my interest in the Civil War has only grown and expanded into other areas of history. This book is my first major project on the Civil War; it was challenging at times but enjoyable. I learned more about the Battles of South Mountain and Antietam than I thought possible. With the focus normally on Gettysburg by many history buffs from around the world, I thought it best to add a volume to the less crowded field of the Maryland Campaign of 1862.

Several people had a direct impact on assisting me with putting together this book. I want to thank the following: author and historian John Michael Priest, who read my manuscript, helped with editing, gave great advice and walked the grounds of Antietam with me; author and historian John Hoptak, who also read my manuscript and offered advice; author and historian D. Scott Hartwig, for answering many questions I had.

Also, thanks go out to the courteous staff members at Antietam National Battlefield and Library who assisted me with finding several letters I needed. Without their help, the search for primary documents would have taken much longer. Special thanks go to the staff at the Wisconsin Veterans Museum, who offered an unlimited amount of assistance and helped me find what I needed.

Finally, to my son, James, who made the journey to Maryland with me while I conducted research to write this book. It was a special moment in my life that I was able to take him to the Hallowed Grounds where so many men fought bravely and gave their lives. I hope the love of history I have may have rubbed off on you, my dear boy.

INTRODUCTION

The cry of war spread like wildfire throughout the South and along the Eastern Seaboard, but the anxiousness and excitement felt by many was not limited to these places. States such as Illinois, Minnesota and Michigan also heard the call of war and prepared to do their part in defending the Union. When the Confederates opened fire on Fort Sumter, the South did more than start a war; it awoke a sleeping giant. On April 12, 1861, Minnesota's governor, Alexander Ramsey, guaranteed to provide President Abraham Lincoln with one thousand men willing to fight for the cause. Wisconsin, not to be outdone by neighboring states, quickly stepped up to aid in the war effort. Between the years of 1861 and 1865, more than ninety-one thousand men from Wisconsin volunteered to fight. On April 16, Governor Alexander Randall published a proclamation to the citizens of Wisconsin asking for any able-bodied man to join the fight to save the Union. "To the Loyal People of Wisconsin: For the first time in the history of this federal government, organized treason has manifested itself within several states of the Union, and armed rebels are making war against it. The proclamation of the President of the United States tells of unlawful combinations too powerful to be suppressed in the ordinary manner and calls for military to sustain him in executing the laws."[1]

The men of Wisconsin enthusiastically and swiftly responded to the call to arms. The-larger-than-expected groups of anxious volunteers signed enlistment papers for a conflict that was not expected to last more than a few months. Shortly after the governor's proclamation was published, the state hired carpenters and ordered them to begin transforming the old fairgrounds near the University of Wisconsin–Madison into a camp for all the new recruits. They named it Camp Randall, the same name it holds today.

While the recruits were excited to share in what was to become the adventure of a lifetime, members of Wisconsin's government saw a problem with so many volunteers joining. With all the eligible men leaving to fight in the war, their families would be left without husbands, fathers and brothers. The war of survival at home could become too great of a burden. So, on the night of April 18, 1861, "at half-past 7:00 p.m., a large gathering of people convened at the Assembly Hall" in Madison. When the meeting was called to order, Madison mayor Chauncey Abbott proposed a call of action for the support of the wives and children of the volunteers. The room filled with loud applause and cheers for Abbott and Governor Randall. Both men made immediate donations of $50 and $200, respectively. Other politicians and businessmen, for the most part, eagerly donated to the cause. The total raised came to $7,490, an equivalent of $214,610 in today's money.[2]

By the time the meeting came to an end around 11:00 p.m., over 1,500 people had shown up to voice their opinions in support of the brave volunteers. The new recruits went to the armory at city hall, where they received uniforms and other equipment. For many, this was a once-in-a-lifetime adventure they did not want to miss. They thought the upcoming fight would last a few months; no one imagined the horrors that lay ahead. The enthusiasm displayed was remarkable; many knew these could be life-changing events but also that, sadly, some would never return home.

Such was the fate of many who enlisted, with the majority thinking the war would not last more than a few months. The ages of the soldiers are mentioned in almost every book written on the Civil War; however, the names of the men who fought and paid with their lives are often overlooked.

With any major study taken on by the author, he or she becomes close to the project. In the case of this book, the situation is no different. I have lived with the men of the 2nd, 3rd, 6th and 7th Wisconsin from Madison, Wisconsin, to Sharpsburg, Maryland. I have read many letters from the soldiers who fought in several battles other than South Mountain and Antietam. Many of the letters did not offer much in the way of information about the battles, making it difficult to know exactly what each of these soldiers experienced; it is even harder to find firsthand accounts from Confederate soldiers.

As a historian, it is my job to search for answers so people who are interested in the Battle of Antietam can get a better understanding of what happened. There is far less material written on Antietam than Gettysburg, making the battle less understood by many. Firsthand accounts are the most important pieces of evidence any historian can find to tell the story of what happened in the small town of Sharpsburg and not just repeat the same information that has been told by the army commanders. Although their stories are important, most generals passed blame to others and do not tell the complete story, in order to make themselves look better. The private who fought, bled and possibly lost a limb had no reason to seek glory, like his superiors. In fact, I personally found it rather frustrating that most of the letters I came across give little to no description of battle.

Most of the soldiers mention the battle with the words "horrors of battle" or state how they "will never forget" what they saw. None of us living today know what life as a Civil War soldier was like or how it felt going through what they did, but it only takes one's imagination to get an idea what hell, horror and pain these men went through. For the men who fought at South Mountain and Antietam and lived, their lives did not get any easier. Within a few short months, Fredericksburg happened, followed by Chancellorsville and then Gettysburg. It was one bloody fight after another; not only did the men from Wisconsin take it in stride, but so did the 19th Indiana and, later, the 24th Michigan. All fought bravely as part of the Iron Brigade. Although I make little mention of the 19th Indiana in this work, it is in no way a sign of a lack of respect for the regiment that fought bravely during the Maryland Campaign of 1862.

It was not my intention to give a step-by-step account of the Battles of South Mountain and Antietam. I leave that honor to other historians, like Stephen Sears, John Hoptek, Scott Hartwig, Ted Alexander and John Priest. This book is not a complete story about what took place at Antietam; rather, it focuses on the role Wisconsin played during that dark day in American history.

The fight at Sharpsburg—the bloodiest single day in American history and a day that many Civil War historians acknowledge as a turning point in the Civil War—thwarted Robert E. Lee's first attempt to move north and bring the war to Northern soil. He had to do this. The war-ravaged South was hurting beyond recovery, and the need for supplies for his army could wait no longer. In part to relieve beleaguered northern Virginia from Federal occupation and to resupply his battered army, Lee crossed into Maryland. He failed but was determined to make another attempt at invasion less than a year later, at Gettysburg.

The Formation of Wisconsin Regiments and Leadership

The 2ND Wisconsin

The 2nd Wisconsin Regiment was organized in Madison during late May and early June 1861. Members of the 2nd Wisconsin signed up to serve for three months, but by June 11 of that year, when the regiment went into Federal service, the government had extended it to a three-year commitment. The regiment consisted of 1,051 officers and enlisted men.

On June 20, 1861, the regiment boarded a train for Washington. The men departed for the capital amid the cheers of those they left behind. After two long days of traveling, the men of the 2nd detrained in Harrisburg, Pennsylvania. They named their temporary bivouac Camp Brady, and the men were finally able to bathe in the Susquehanna River and pitch tents and cook rations.

On Sunday, June 23, the rested soldiers were armed with Harpers Ferry muskets and given forty rounds of "buck and ball" cartridges. The next day, they boarded a train and finished their journey to Washington and from there went to Camp Meridian Hill, in the northern part of Washington. They remained in place until July 2 before moving across the Potomac River into Virginia. There they stayed two miles outside of Fort Corcoran, setting up camp and engaging in more drilling until they received orders to move out. The Confederate army was close, and the Union army was to meet them head-on at Manassas Junction. On July 16, they cooked rations and shouldered arms; battle was around the corner, and the soldiers of the 2nd Wisconsin prepared for their first fight, which would come on July 21, 1861, at the First Battle of Bull Run in Manassas, Virginia.[3]

The regiment constantly drilled until orders came from Washington, D.C., to move out and join up with General Irvin McDowell's Army of Northeast Virginia. Military life was not all business for some. In the evenings, some men took part in drinking whiskey and playing cards, which became the biggest form of entertainment and would be a common complaint from residents near Camp Randall. Local farmers even reported that a few of their chickens went missing. The raid on Voight's Brewery from a group of soldiers was to be the last straw. From June 10 on, no one was allowed outside of Camp Randall.

Captain Wilson Colwell of Company B was from La Crosse and was considered one of the strongest men of the regiment. Before the war, he had been in the finance business, specializing in large commercial business purchases, with which he was successful. When the war broke out, Colwell jumped at the opportunity to fight for the cause and preserve the United States. He was known by those who crossed paths with him as a "true gentleman, a thorough disciplinarian and a brave soldier."[4]

Lucius Fairchild came to live in Madison with his parents in 1846 and remained there for three years until moving west for the gold rush.

Petersburg, Virginia. Camp of 2nd Wisconsin Infantry. *Library of Congress.*

General Lucius Fairchild, 2nd Wisconsin Regiment. *Library of Congress*.

He remained out there until 1855, when he returned home and began studying law. Five years later, in 1860, he was accepted by the state bar association. When the war started, he was appointed captain of the 1st Wisconsin, but he later accepted command of the 2nd Wisconsin on August 30, 1862, with the rank of colonel. During the Civil War, Fairchild led the 2nd Wisconsin at the Second Battle of Bull Run, Antietam, Chancellorsville and Gettysburg, where he was shot in the left arm, resulting in amputation. After he was mustered out of service, Fairchild returned home and went on to have a political career.

The 2nd Wisconsin Infantry was involved in more than forty types of engagements during their time in service. They were part of one of the most famous brigades in the Federal army, known as the Iron Brigade. Throughout the Civil War, the 2nd Wisconsin took part in heavy combat and suffered high losses in several engagements. Total losses were 315 men, with 10 officers and 228 enlisted men killed; 77 men alone died from disease.

The 3ʳᵈ Wisconsin

On June 19, 1861, the 3ʳᵈ Wisconsin Infantry organized at Camp Hamilton in Fond du Lac and mustered into Federal service on June 29. The soldiers from the 3ʳᵈ remained in Fond du Lac, where they received gear and other equipment and drilled until leaving Wisconsin for Hagerstown, Maryland, on July 12, 1861. Once there, the 3ʳᵈ was sent to Harpers Ferry, and by August 20, it had relocated to Darnestown, Maryland.

Thomas H. Ruger was born in Lima, New York, in April 1833. In 1844, the Ruger family moved to Janesville, Wisconsin, where they would remain for the rest of their lives. Thomas Ruger entered the Military Academy at West Point in 1850 and graduated in 1854. At West Point, Thomas performed well in all subjects and, by the time he graduated, ranked second in his class. On graduation, Ruger left West Point with the rank of second lieutenant and was assigned to the U.S. Army Corps of Engineers, where he served under Major P.G.T. Beauregard. He remained in his position at Fort Jackson in New Orleans until he resigned his commission and returned to Janesville in the summer of 1855.

Not long after returning to Janesville, Ruger discovered that he had an interest in law and continued educating himself until 1857, when he was admitted to the bar. He opened his own law business, becoming successful. He continued practicing until the war broke out in 1861. Within hours of hearing the news about the Confederate attack on Fort Sumter, Ruger offered his services to the War Department.[5]

Governor Randall wasted no time in asking Ruger to travel to Madison and assist with forming troops for the defense of the Union. Ruger accepted; he left his law practice and began work right away. Randall gave Ruger the position of engineer in chief on his staff with the rank of brigadier general. However, Ruger wanted to serve his time on active duty and accepted the demotion to the rank of lieutenant colonel. The 3ʳᵈ Wisconsin's colonel, Charles Hamilton, shortly after accepting command, was promoted to brigadier general; this allowed Governor Randall to promote Lieutenant Colonel Ruger to the rank of full colonel, which he maintained until leaving the army in 1863.

The 3ʳᵈ remained in Darnestown with little to do but drill and engage in normal camp duties. Orders were received to move to the town of Frederick, Maryland, on September 12, 1861, to stop a local group of legislators from attempting to hold a vote for Maryland to leave the Union. They succeeded, and the 3ʳᵈ Wisconsin Infantry remained in Frederick until the spring of

1862, except for three companies that were sent to Harpers Ferry in October to gather a stockpile of corn needed to feed the men. The foray resulted in Companies A, C and H seeing their first action on October 16.[6]

About sixteen hundred Confederate soldiers consisting of infantry, cavalry and artillery skirmished with the small elements of the Union army at Bolivar Heights. The 3rd was the heaviest engaged in the fight and stood their ground until the Confederates retreated. The 3rd had four men killed and seven wounded.

By March 1862, the 3rd was on the move again under the command of Major General Nathaniel Banks's Fifth Army Corps. Between March 1862 and September of the same year, the 3rd Wisconsin would be under different commands. By the time the Maryland Campaign began on September 5, 1862, the hard-fighting 3rd Wisconsin Infantry was assigned to the Third Brigade, First Division, Twelfth Corps, Army of the Potomac.

The 6th Wisconsin

The 6th Wisconsin Infantry mustered into the United States Army at Camp Randall in Madison, Wisconsin, on July 16, 1861. Shortly after, the 1,045-troop regiment left by rail for the nation's capital on July 28. After arriving in Washington on August 7, they set up camp just outside of the city. The regiment was armed with Belgian muskets—a heavy, clumsy gun of large caliber and nothing in comparison to the Springfield rifled musket.

Brigadier General Edward S. Bragg lived in Fond du Lac, where he practiced law. When the war began in 1861, Bragg believed in preserving the Union and assisted in raising troops in his home city. He was able to organize a full company of men and was given the commission of captain. After leaving Wisconsin with his new troops, he was promoted to major on September 17, 1861. Showing an impressive skill for military life, Bragg was promoted to lieutenant colonel on June 20, 1862. He remained in the service until Confederate general Robert E. Lee surrendered his army in 1865.[7]

Rufus Dawes was born in 1839 in Ohio but moved to Mauston in 1855 with his father and brother. Dawes spent much of his young life moving between Wisconsin and Ohio. When the war broke out in 1861, the twenty-two-year-old Dawes joined Company K, 6th Wisconsin. He was able to assemble many recruits—not short-term, like many other people, but for the duration of the war. Over the span of the war, he made a name for himself,

General Edward
S. Bragg. *Library
of Congress.*

rising through the ranks as the war went on. By war's end, he held the rank
of brevet brigadier general and was looked on as an important leader in the
Iron Brigade.

From the time the 6th Wisconsin arrived in Washington through March
1862, it remained in the district to guard the city against Confederate attack.
By March 10, 1862, its camp was broken up. The entire Army of the Potomac
was on the move toward Centerville, Virginia, where it expected to give battle.
The men camped just outside of Fairfax Court House, where many soldiers
wrote wills and farewell letters to their families. The expected battle never
occurred. Word spread on March 11, 1862, that the Rebel army had left
Centerville and Manassas. the Army of the Potomac would just have to wait.[8]

The 6th Wisconsin Infantry remained with the Army of the Potomac until
the Confederate army surrendered at Appomattox in 1865. The 6th would
not see its first real combat until August 28, 1862, at the Second Battle of
Manassas. By war's end, the regiment had lost 357 men, of whom 228 were
killed in action and 112 died from disease.[9]

THE 7TH WISCONSIN

On September 2, 1861, at Camp Randall in Madison, the 7th Wisconsin became the last regiment to join the Iron Brigade. The 973 men of the 7th were sent to Washington, D.C., on that date and arrived there on October 1 under the command of General Rufus King. They remained with the same brigade until the end of the war.

Captain John B. Callis, originally from North Carolina, had moved to Lancaster, Wisconsin, before the Civil War began. He enlisted in the military in 1861 and quickly rose to the rank of captain of Company F, 7th Wisconsin Infantry. During the Battle of Antietam, he led his men into the bloody cornfield and, later, fought with bravery at the Battle of Gettysburg, where he was severely wounded. That wound forced him to resign his commission from the regular army, but he later received a promotion to lieutenant colonel in the Veteran's Reserve Corps in 1865. Because of his leadership skills, Callis, when mustered out of service, received the rank of brigadier general.

After the war, Callis returned to the South, to Alabama, where he became a congressman and served for several years before deciding to return to Wisconsin, where he became active in Tom Cox Post No. 132 of the Grand Army of the Republic.

From October 1861 to August 1862, the 7th mainly drilled before setting out with the Army of the Potomac into Virginia. It was not until August 28, 1862, that the 7th took part in its first major fight, at Gainesville, Virginia. When the Civil War came to an end, the 7th Wisconsin had lost a total of 424 men—10 officers and 271 men killed in action and 143 enlisted men dying of disease.[10]

2

SEPTEMBER 1862

THE ARMIES MOVE

THE ARMY OF NORTHERN VIRGINIA

With the devastating blow dealt to the Union army at the Second Battle of Bull Run, it looked like the Confederacy could win the war. General Robert E. Lee's Army of Northern Virginia seemed invincible. Since given command earlier in 1862, Lee had been on the offensive. Throughout two months, he defeated two Union armies in Virginia and now had plans to move north into Maryland for what would become known as the Maryland Campaign of 1862.

General Lee thought that by moving into Northern territory his army could get the needed supplies and pull the Union army away from Richmond and out of northern Virginia. A successful invasion could also have a bearing on the upcoming federal congressional elections. On September 2, the Confederate army prepared three days' rations to hold its soldiers over until they moved farther north. By sunrise the following day, Lee's army prepared to advance. Soon after, Lee sent for his military secretary, Armistead Long. Unable to write after spraining his wrists and breaking a small bone in one hand following an accident with his horse at Second Bull Run, Lee dictated the dispatch to Long.

In the dispatch to Confederate president Jefferson Davis, Lee argued that the time was right to enter Maryland, since the Union army had been beaten and demoralized. Now, according to Lee, was the time to strike!

General Robert E. Lee.
Library of Congress.

Although Lee admitted that his troops were not "properly equipped for invasion"—they lacked much-needed supplies such as shoes, proper clothing and adequate transportation (the "animals being much reduced")—he believed that sitting still was not something he could afford to do.[11]

"It was decided to cross the Potomac east of the Blue Ridge, in order, by threatening Washington and Baltimore, to cause the enemy to withdraw from the south bank, where his presence endangered our communications and the safety of those engaged in the removal of our wounded and the captured property from the late battlefields," wrote General Lee in his report dated August 19, 1863. At the time of the Maryland invasion, Lee had around fifty-five thousand troops combined.[12]

Lee thought his move into Maryland would allow citizens to gain their liberties back and perhaps side with the Confederacy. "Some additions to our ranks will no doubt be received," Lee wrote Davis. More than confident that Davis would approve of his plan, Lee did not wait for a response. Instead, he ordered his men to march on September 4 with General D.H. Hill's division in the lead. Generals Thomas "Stonewall" Jackson and James Longstreet continued marching on to Leesburg and crossed the Potomac at White's Ford and continued to Frederick.[13]

Prior to leaving Leesburg, Lee issued orders barring most of the sick, wounded and barefoot men from marching to Maryland and diverted them toward Winchester. This order greatly reduced Lee's army strength by approximately fifteen thousand fighting men. Several hundred shoeless infantrymen moved south of Leesburg and passed by the idle 3rd Virginia Cavalry. This alarmed Lieutenant Robert T. Hubard, who watched in awe as squads of soldiers ripped off their shoes and tossed them.[14]

General Jeb Stuart's cavalry, with Fitzhugh Lee's brigade in advance, followed Jackson across the Potomac to protect the infantry's movements until Jackson was at Harpers Ferry. Stuart's troopers encountered Union cavalry on the afternoon of September 5 near Poolesville, capturing large numbers of Union prisoners. It was a quick fight that resulted in few casualties for Stuart. "The reception of our troops in Maryland was attended with the greatest demonstrations of joy, and the hope of enabling the inhabitants to throw off the tyrant's yoke stirred every Southern heart with renewed vigor and enthusiasm," Stuart wrote.[15]

By September 7, all of Lee's army had crossed the Potomac and were camped either at or near Maryland's second-largest city, Frederick, less than fifty miles northwest of Washington, D.C. Lee had high hopes that his northern invasion would succeed, but his army was in poor condition. His men were worn out from all the marching and hunger. All of this concerned Lee, but the large number of stragglers alarmed him. To combat that, on September 4, Lee ordered R.H. Chilton, his assistant adjutant-general, to draft General Orders No. 102, which stated: "A provost guard, under direction of Brigadier General L.A. Armistead, will follow in rear of the army, arrest stragglers, and punish summarily all depredators, and keep the men with their commands. Commanders of brigades will cause rear guards to be placed under charge of efficient officers in rear of their brigades, to prevent the men from leaving the ranks, right, left, front, or rear, this officer being held by brigade commanders to a strict accountability for proper performance of this duty."[16]

With a plan in place to help slow the process of straggling, the less-than-warm reception Lee's army received by the Marylanders disappointed Jefferson Davis. While no hostilities had been shown against Lee, he was by far more concerned about achieving his goals on a military level; Lee continued with his plan of invasion. Now with the comfort of having most of his army safely across the Potomac and his men somewhat rested from their time in or around Frederick, Lee gave the order to march. His order was to move west of Frederick, over the Catoctin and South Mountain ranges and into the valley of the Cumberland, where he could open his line of communication and supplies. Two small garrisons of Union troops remained in the valley, however. One was at Martinsburg (about three thousand men under the command of General Julius White); the other was at Harpers Ferry (ten thousand strong under the command of Colonel Dixon Miles). Finding out that Union soldiers were present was not a shock to Lee, but what did surprise him was that they did not leave once his army crossed the Potomac into Maryland. Hagerstown was the targeted spot to rest and gain supplies, and this movement would threaten Pennsylvania, forcing the Union army farther from Washington.

On the night of September 9, Lee met with Generals Walker and Jackson and drew up a plan on how he wanted these Union troops handled. General Longstreet did not attend the initial meeting but happened to walk by Lee's tent. "As I had not been called, I turned to go away when General Lee, recognizing my voice, called me in," Longstreet recalled. He was then briefed on the planned movements for the upcoming days. On the morning of September 10, Jackson proceeded with his command toward Martinsburg. After forcing the Union garrison to retreat or surrender there, he was to move down the south side of the Potomac and attack Harpers Ferry. General Lafayette McLaws with his division, along with R.H. Anderson's division, was ordered to seize Maryland Heights on the north side of the Potomac. Brigadier General John Walker was ordered to seize Loudoun Heights on the east side of the Shenandoah, where it converges with the Potomac River. After taking control of Harpers Ferry, Jackson, McLaws and Walker were ordered to join the rest of the army at Boonsboro or Hagerstown.[17]

Longstreet's command, along with the army's supply and baggage, was to follow behind Jackson until reaching Boonsboro. General D.H. Hill's division was to follow as a rear guard behind Longstreet, and General Stuart and his cavalry would remain east of the mountains to observe enemy troop

Major General George B. McClellan, commander of the Army of the Potomac during the Maryland Campaign. *Library of Congress.*

movements. Everything was falling into place until Lee received word that Federal troops were on the move toward Hagerstown from Chambersburg, so Longstreet received orders to move to secure the road at Williamsport and protect the approach to Hagerstown.

Knowing the army was worn out, hungry and poorly clothed, Longstreet disagreed with the plan. The dividing of his army into five parts in largely pro-Union western Maryland was hazardous. After the meeting, Colonel Chilton drafted the orders of operation and distributed them to Longstreet, McLaws, D.H. Hill, Jackson, Stuart and Walker. Special Orders 191 became some of the most famous Confederate orders of the Civil War, as they contained Lee's plan of dividing his army. The following are Lee's orders:

SPECIAL ORDERS No. 191.
HDQRS. ARMY OF NORTHERN VIRGINIA,
September 9, 1862.
I. The citizens of Fredericktown being unwilling, while overrun by members of his army, to open their stores, in order to give them confidence,

and to secure to officers and men purchasing supplies for benefit of this command, all officers and men of this army are strictly prohibited from visiting Fredericktown except on business, in which case they will bear evidence of this in writing from division commanders. The provost-marshal in Fredericktown will see that his guard rigidly enforces this order.

II. Major Taylor will proceed to Leesburg, Va., and arrange for transportation of the sick and those unable to walk to Winchester, securing the transportation of the country for this purpose. The route between this and Culpeper Court-House east of the mountains being unsafe will no longer be traveled. Those on the way to this army already across the river will move up promptly; all others will proceed to Winchester collectively and under command of officers, at which point, being the general depot of this army, its movements will be known, and instructions given by commanding officer regulating further movements.

III. The army will resume its march tomorrow, taking the Hagerstown road. General Jackson's command will form the advance, and, after passing Middletown, with such portion as he may select, take the route toward Sharpsburg, cross the Potomac at the most convenient point, and by Friday morning take possession of the Baltimore and Ohio Railroad, capture such of them as may be at Martinsburg, and intercept such as may attempt to escape from Harper's Ferry.

IV. General Longstreet's command will pursue the main road as far as Boonsboro, where it will halt, with reserve, supply, and baggage trains of the army.

V. General McLaws, with his own division and that of General R.H. Anderson, will follow General Longstreet. On reaching Middletown will take the route to Harper's Ferry, and by Friday morning possess himself of the Maryland Heights and endeavor to capture the enemy at Harper's Ferry and vicinity.

VI. General Walker, with his division, after accomplishing the object in which he is now engaged, will cross the Potomac at Cheek's Ford, ascend its right bank to Lovettsville, take possession of Loudoun Heights, if practicable, by Friday morning, Keys' Ford on his left, and the road between the end of the mountain and the Potomac on his right. He will, as far as practicable, co-operate with Generals McLaws and Jackson, and intercept retreat of the enemy.

VII. General D.H. Hill's division will form the rear guard of the army, pursuing the road taken by the main body. The reserve artillery, ordnance, and supply trains, &c. will precede General Hill.

VIII. General Stuart will detach a squadron of cavalry to accompany the commands of Generals Longstreet, Jackson, and McLaws, and, with the main body of the cavalry, will cover the route of the army, bringing up all stragglers that may have been left behind.

IX. The commands of Generals Jackson, McLaws, and Walker, after accomplishing the objects for which they have been detached, will join the main body of the army at Boonsboro or Hagerstown.

X. Each regiment on the march will habitually carry its axes in the regimental ordnance wagons, for use of the men at their encampments, to procure wood, &c.

By command of General R.E. Lee:

R. H. CHILTON,

Assistant Adjutant-General.

Lee believed time was on his side, but that was not the case. The Union army thought to be in Washington had left and was closer than he anticipated. Poor intelligence from Lee's cavalry commander, Jeb Stuart, left Lee in the dark. He could not account for the thirteen hundred Union cavalry between the two locations Lee mentioned in his special orders. His orders were already falling apart before an attempt to execute them occurred.

The Army of the Potomac, already on the march, was more than ten miles from Washington and had skirmished with Confederate cavalry at Pooleville and Hyattstown. By September 9, the Army of the Potomac's advance was between Washington and Frederick, on the heels of the Army of Northern Virginia, whose tail end was still in Frederick on September 11. Lee expected his army to move more quickly than possible to carry out the orders, but it was difficult to march fast without proper footwear. "Most of our marches were on graveled turnpike roads, which were very severe on the barefooted men and cut up their feet horribly," wrote Private Spencer G. Welch of the 13th Virginia Infantry. Barefoot or not, the army had to move faster.[18]

General Jackson left Frederick before daylight on the morning of September 10, heading west. Jackson's troops crossed Catoctin and South Mountain before noon. The fast movements quickly wore his men out; therefore, he ordered his men to halt just outside of Boonsboro. The men rested for the remainder of the day, just thirteen miles from Frederick. The next day, September 11, Jackson crossed the Potomac near Williamsport. From there, he divided his army, ordering General A.P. Hill to take his division directly to Martinsburg. Jackson would attack the Union troops from

General Robert E. Lee, seated.
Library of Congress.

the north and the west. There was to be no resistance from the Yankees, who fled Martinsburg on hearing of Jackson's approach. Jackson captured Martinsburg the following day along with a few prisoners and supplies. Twenty-four hours later, he marched his command toward Harpers Ferry.

Behind Jackson's command came General Longstreet, who, by the time Jackson's men crossed the Potomac, had halted in Boonsboro. News of Federal troops approaching Hagerstown from the direction of Chambersburg forced Longstreet to move his men toward Hagerstown quickly to seize the large amounts of flour there. Union troops, marching south from Chambersburg, also threatened Jackson from behind. Longstreet's movement to Hagerstown protected Jackson from attack, but stretched Lee's army even further, altering the orders spelled out in 191.

Longstreet's command arrived in Hagerstown on September 12, with the news that the Federals had fled Martinsburg to Harpers Ferry. Lee had to neutralize Harpers Ferry, as it placed a large Federal garrison along his possible line of retreat into Virginia. Jackson continued his march and reached Bolivar Heights, west of Harpers Ferry, by Saturday, September

13. Generals McLaws and Walker were still on the move toward their ordered locations, but both had fallen behind schedule. On the afternoon of September 13, McLaws finally gained possession of Maryland Heights, and Walker took control of Loudoun Heights. The Confederates had Union colonel Dixon Miles and his soldiers surrounded at Harpers Ferry.

To prevent Union troops at Harpers Ferry from escaping, Lee ordered D.H. Hill to move toward Boonsboro. Hill, receiving word from Stuart that two brigades of Union soldiers were not far behind, decided to send two brigades led by General Samuel Garland and Colonel Alfred Colquitt to guard Fox's and Turner's Gap at South Mountain. Hill's other three brigades went to Boonsboro. Longstreet's new orders were to move his command to aid Hill near Boonsboro. When Longstreet's command neared Boonsboro on September 14, 1862, the men heard the sound of guns rumbling in the distance. By the time Longstreet arrived, he found Hill heavily engaged in a fierce fight against Union troops. The Battle of South Mountain had already begun.

THE ARMY OF THE POTOMAC

The loss at Second Bull Run gave President Lincoln and his administration a cause for alarm, necessitating another change in command. On September 2, 1862, Lincoln, along with General Henry Halleck, arrived at the home of Major General George B. McClellan. Lincoln discussed his opinions on the latest troubles of the Union army, and Halleck offered to restore McClellan to command. "Again, I have been called upon to save the country," McClellan wrote his wife on September 5, 1862. The Federal soldiers rejoiced. For Lincoln, however, placing McClellan back in command was a difficult choice. Halleck had to inform McClellan; Lincoln could not bring himself to speak the words.

General McClellan began right away and worked vigorously, putting in place his field army. He assembled a force of sixty thousand troops and 313 guns consisting of five corps, two detached divisions and a cavalry division. He accomplished this between September 3 and September 6. The Army of the Potomac, much like the Army of Northern Virginia, faced some of the same problems with straggling and lack of discipline. Unlike Lee's army, the Army of the Potomac was better equipped with the supplies needed to fight.

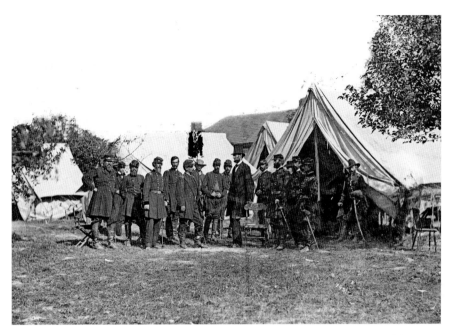

President Lincoln, General McClellan and staff after the Battle of Antietam. *Library of Congress*.

Before leaving Washington, McClellan took time preparing the defenses of Washington. By September 5, he had ordered the First Corps under Major General Joseph Hooker—an arrogant, highly ambitious man who liked to criticize his superiors constantly—and the Ninth Corps, led by Major General Jesse L. Reno, to push forward, forming the right wing of the army under the command of Major General Ambrose Burnside. The army's center wing consisted of the Second Corps, led by Major General Edwin Sumner, and the Twelfth Corps, led by Major General Alpheus S. Williams. Sumner was to command the center, while Major General William Franklin took command of the left wing, which was his own Sixth Corps plus Darius Couch's division, to aid in the support.[19]

By September 7, McClellan had ridden out of Washington with hopes of crushing Lee's Army of Northern Virginia. The right wing of the army moved north to prevent the Confederates from threatening moving on Baltimore, while Sumner pushed northwest toward the city of Frederick. General Franklin's men moved to the south, hugging the Potomac River. McClellan set out from Washington with no exact idea where Lee was or where he was headed. His army moved slowly for the first several days, keeping their eyes and ears open and waiting to hear the next order. "The

Left: General Joseph Hooker. *Library of Congress*.

Right: Portrait of Major General William B. Franklin, officer of the Federal army. *Library of Congress*.

object of these movements was to feel the enemy; to compel him to develop his intentions," wrote McClellan.[20]

With the roads to Washington and Baltimore covered, McClellan continued his advance toward Frederick. By September 11, his army was within a short distance of Frederick with the tail end of Lee's army in the process of moving to the west. Burnside led his right wing toward Frederick on the morning of the eleventh, and by evening, he had two divisions at Ridgeville with another three miles north of Damascus heading toward Ridgeville. Burnside proceeded with caution, since the Confederates could still occupy Frederick. Brigadier General Jacob Cox, commander of the Fourth Division, Ninth Corps, never received any such communication. Unaware of the dangers ahead, he led the division into Frederick, where General Wade Hampton's much smaller Confederate cavalry force attacked him on Patrick Street. Two of Cox's men were killed and seven were taken prisoner in the short skirmish.[21]

The next morning, Brigadier General Alfred Pleasonton's Union cavalry left Frederick ahead of the Ninth Corps. The objective was to clear out any Confederates between Frederick and Pleasant Valley. McClellan ordered the First, Second and Twelfth Corps to move and mass around Frederick. Franklin received orders to cross the Monocacy River and take possession of Buckeystown, about five miles south of Frederick. With this move complete, the Army of the Potomac was poised to move in any direction.[22]

With his cavalry and Ninth Corps on the move and the rest of the army converging on Frederick, McClellan set up his headquarters there. On the morning of September 13, members of the First Division of the Twelfth Corps camped in a meadow on the outskirts of Frederick—in the same spot where the Confederate army had camped days before. As it happened, skirmishers of the 27th Indiana found a spot in the

Major General Alfred Pleasonton of the Union army in uniform. *Library of Congress.*

meadow that pleased them and set up to boil coffee. While relaxing, one soldier saw some paper aying in the tall grass; he discovered a sheet of paper wrapped around three cigars. The cigars alone were a prize, but a closer examination of the papers' contents revealed something unbelievable.

Immediately, the soldier went to turn his find over to his commanding officer, who, after reading it, sent it by messenger to General McClellan. McClellan could not believe his eyes. In his hand he held a copy of General Robert E. Lee's Special Orders 191. "While at Frederick, on the 13th, I obtained reliable information of the movements and intentions of the enemy, which made it clear that it was necessary to force the passage of the South Mountain range and gain possession of Boonsboro and Rohrersville before any relief could be afforded to Harpers Ferry," wrote McClellan.[23]

McClellan sent a telegram to President Lincoln, stating, "I have the whole rebel force in front of me but am confident, and no time shall be lost." He continued, "I think Lee has made a gross mistake, and that he will be severely punished for it." While Orders 191 were authentic, McClellan ran into a bit of a problem, as the orders appeared to have been drafted on September 9. Jackson, according to the orders, was to take control of

Harpers Ferry by September 12. Not knowing if this had happened yet, McClellan dragged his feet once again. He sent a copy of Lee's orders to his cavalry commander and ordered him to follow the route and see if indeed Lee had followed it.[24]

The rumbling of cannon fire in the direction of Harpers Ferry made McClellan think the direction of travel in Orders 191 was correct and that Lee had fallen behind schedule. Hearing news from Colonel Miles on the morning of the thirteenth that the Confederates possessed the heights surrounding Harpers Ferry, McClellan would "relieve the place" as quickly as he could. It was clear that Lee had divided his army.

By nightfall on September 13, McClellan had his plan of attack ready. The majority of the Army of the Potomac, led by the Ninth Corps, was to move toward South Mountain using the National Pike, heading west of Frederick toward the direction where the main Confederate body was thought to be. McClellan figured that Longstreet's and Hill's commands were still in Boonsboro, but he would not have known Longstreet had already moved toward Hagerstown, leaving Hill alone. With the Ninth Corps leading the way, followed by Hooker's First Corps, followed by Sumner's center wing, McClellan wanted to attack the main Confederate body head-on while Franklin's command attacked from the south.[25]

McClellan was confident his plan of attack would work and was anxious to put his men into motion. Lee had received reports not only from General Stuart but also from D.H. Hill that McClellan's army had marched from Frederick. On the night of September 13, General Alfred Colquitt, at Turner's Gap on South Mountain, prepared for what was to become a bigger fight than Stuart had led Lee to believe was coming. The battle for South Mountain was starting.[26]

CLASH AT SOUTH MOUNTAIN

Although most of the Wisconsin regiments fought at Turner's Gap, it is important to briefly summarize what else happened to the Army of the Potomac at South Mountain. The Maryland Campaign of 1862 did not go as planned.

CRAMPTON'S GAP

Major General William B. Franklin's Sixth Corps rose at 5:50 a.m. on September 14, 1862, and marched from Jefferson to Burkittsville. Major General George McClellan issued orders to Franklin, along with the assistance of Major General Darius Couch's Division of the Fourth Corps, to secure Crampton's Gap. At Jefferson, Franklin waited for Couch to arrive, but upon learning that Couch had fallen farther behind than anticipated, Franklin did not wait. Not wanting to let General Lee slip past, Franklin continued toward Crampton's Gap.

Franklin's Corps consisted of about thirteen thousand men in the six brigades that made up the corps' two divisions. Most of the soldiers of the Sixth Corps were veterans who had seen little to no combat in the last few months. By the time the Battle of South Mountain came, they were well rested and ready to fight. Both division commanders, Major General Henry Slocum and Major General William F. Smith, were West Point graduates. Within a year, both would command their own corps.

Slocum's First Division led the march, with Colonel Henry L. Cake's 96th Pennsylvania (Third Brigade) at the head. Franklin, however, was unaware that his corps' movements had been observed by the Confederates. McClellan had ordered Franklin to move out at first light and take control of the gap if it proved not to be heavily defended. If it was, Franklin was to mass his columns and attack. One can imagine what the terribly outnumbered Confederates thought as that massive Union force of thirteen thousand drew closer. They were too spread out along South Mountain, not knowing which gap the Union army would attack.

Confederate colonel William Allen Parham was ordered to take his three regiments and battery to guard Crampton's Gap. If needed, Parham was instructed to use the 10th Georgia, under the command of Major Willis C. Holt, to guard the Rohrersville Road. When Parham's regiments reached their position on the gap, they met up with Colonel Thomas Munford's cavalry, which had been patrolling the area for over a day now.

It was close to noon when a small detachment of cavalry from the 6th Pennsylvania ahead of Franklin's corps ran into Munford's pickets at Burkittsville. It was not much of a fight. The 6th turned and rode back,

The Battle of South Mountain, Maryland. Sunday, September 14, 1862. *Library of Congress.*

reporting their encounter to Colonel Cake (96th Pennsylvania). Cake ordered companies A and F from his regiment forward as skirmishers. Munford's pickets put up a fight, utilizing every form of cover they came across until the Pennsylvanians pushed them through town. Cake's skirmishers continued forward, firing as fast as possible. They halted just outside of town when Munford's pickets reached the main Confederate battle line behind a stone wall at the base of South Mountain along the Mountain Church Road. The remaining companies of the 96th Pennsylvania marched to the eastern edge of Burkittsville and took a position along the Knoxville Road, where "they were completely concealed from the view of the enemy and covered from the fire of his artillery."[27]

Confederate artillery from Lieutenant Colonel R. Preston Chew's battery below Crampton's Gap, along with Captain Basil Charles Manly's North Carolina battery from Brownsville Gap, just to the south, lobbed several shots at the Sixth Corps, with little to no effect. To ease the pressure, Slocum ordered Captain John C. Wolcott's 1st Maryland Battery to move up and answer the Confederates with his guns until a battle plan could be devised. Until then, the men were able to eat some of their rations and rest. Slocum did not know how thin the Confederate line of battle was to his front. While Slocum prepared to attack, Munford was prepared to receive an attack; he posted the 6th, 12th and 16th Virginia Regiments of Mahone's brigade under Colonel Parham as his line of defense on the Mountain Church Road. The 6th, 12th, 16th and 41st Virginia Regiments were posted behind stone walls and rail fences along the road on the eastern base side of the mountain. To the right of the Confederate line was the 2nd Virginia Cavalry and, on the left, the 12th Virginia Cavalry; members of both had dismounted and acted as sharpshooters.[28]

All in all, Munford had about twelve hundred men to defend the gap against the thirteen thousand men of Franklin's corps; however, Munford had the advantage of position and more artillery. He also had his men in place and was prepared for an attack, unlike the advancing Slocum. After a reconnaissance conducted by Slocum's Division, it was determined that Colonel Joseph J. Bartlett would lead the advance. The attack was to be made on the Confederate right and flank of the Arnoldstown Road leading over the mountain. Bartlett organized his brigade as secretly as possible, under cover from artillery "to a large field near its base, where the column of attack was to be formed, each brigade in two lines, at 200 paces in the rear." By 3:00 p.m., the final attack column was formed in the following order: the 27th Regiment New York Volunteers deployed as skirmishers; behind the 27th, by two hundred yards, the 5th Maine and 16th New York Volunteers in line of battle; and the brigades of General Newton and Colonel Torbert, each brigade being in two lines. "The regiments in line of battle and the lines 200 yards from each other; the 96th Pennsylvania Volunteers, of Bartlett's brigade, which had advanced into the village, formed in rear, and joined the column as it advanced; the 121st New York Volunteers was held as a reserve at the point where the column was formed."[29]

It was 4:00 p.m. when the 27th New York's skirmishers advanced. Chew's battery opened with a heavy and well-directed fire, without stopping. The skirmishers also battled the bright sun in their eyes until they neared the base of the mountain, where the high trees gave some—albeit short-lived—relief. As soon as they reached shade, they came under heavy musketry fire from Munford and Parham's men from the trees and behind the stone wall providing them "admirable cover." Their advance halted at a rail fence about three hundred yards from the Confederate line, and the skirmishers withdrew. Now that the Confederate line had been found and their strength known, Slocum brought in his main battle line, and the deadly fight ensued.[30]

The stone wall behind which the Confederates sheltered hampered Bartlett's advance. Seeing the difficulties, Slocum ordered the artillery to move up fast and blast Munford's men out. A battery came as fast as possible, but by the time it was set up, Munford's troops had abandoned their position and retreated up the mountain. Bartlett's brigade followed in close pursuit and took cover once Munford's men reached the crest of the hill and opened with small-arms fire. Confederate brigadier general Howell Cobb moved into position to aid Munford and sent two of his strongest regiments to Munford's assistance. They had hardly formed a line when a message was received from Parham that Union troops were overwhelming his position and requested support at the double quick. Cobb sent his two remaining regiments to Parham, with Cobb himself followed along. McLaws had impressed upon Cobb, Munford and Parham the importance of the Confederate position before he advanced to Harpers Ferry. His orders of holding the gap at all costs meant just that. "I must hold the gap if it cost the life of every man in my command," Cobb wrote.[31]

When he reached the top of the mountain, Cobb found that Bartlett's men had been repulsed and driven "back in the center and had been pursued down the other side of the mountain by Parham's brigade." He soon discovered, however, "that the enemy, by their greatly superior numbers, were flanking us both upon the right and left. Two of my regiments were sent to the right and two to the left to meet these movements of the enemy. In this we were successful, until the center gave way, pressed by fresh troops of the enemy and increased numbers. Up to this time the troops had fought well and maintained their ground against greatly superior forces."[32]

Cobb wrote in his report dated September 22, 1862, the following:

> *The Tenth Georgia Regiment, of General Semmes' brigade, had been ordered to the gap from their position at the foot of the mountain and participated in the battle with great courage and energy. After the lines were broken, all my efforts to rally the troops were unsuccessful. I was enabled to check their advance by momentary rallies, and, the night coming on, I made a successful stand near the foot of the mountain, which position we held during the night, and until a new position was taken about day-dawn the next morning, in the rear of Brownsville, which position was held until the surrender of Harpers Ferry. General Semmes' brigade and Wilcox's brigade, under the command of Colonel Cumming, of the Tenth Georgia Regiment, had been ordered, the former by General Semmes, the latter by yourself, to my support. They came up to the position I occupied during the night; they could not have reached me sooner. The whole number of troops engaged on our side did not exceed 2,200, whilst the force of the enemy was variously estimated from 10,000 to 20,000 men. It could not have been less than 10,000 and probably reached 15,000.*[33]

With darkness fast approaching and exhaustion setting it, the Union forces halted. Out of cartridges and fatigued with the attack having taken its toll on the troops, both sides fought hard, but in the end, Slocum's men scattered the Confederate defenders. The fight for Crampton's Gap resulted in a Union victory, but it did not come easy. The Confederates, as was the norm, had performed well and fought hard defending their position. The Union victory resulted in 113 killed, 418 wounded and 2 missing for a total of 533. The loss the Confederates had is a little sketchy. General Cobb stated, "It is impossible for me to report the casualties, as the fate of only a few of the large number missing is certainly known."[34]

While Franklin's Sixth Corps was engaged in combat at Crampton's Gap, Burnside's First and Ninth Corps were battling it out six miles northeast at Turner's and Fox's Gap.

FOX'S GAP

General D.H. Hill was up early on the morning of September 14. The sun had just begun rising when he, along with some of his staff, rode up Turner's Gap. He was following Lee's orders to prepare a defense on South Mountain to block the Yankee army's advance. Hill believed the morning ride proved to be of value, writing that Fox's Gap "satisfied me that it could only be held by a large force." Hill had been busy since receiving his orders from Lee. Since arriving in Boonsboro, he had watched and waited for any indication that trouble for the Southern army was happening at Harpers Ferry. Although Hill had a lot on his plate—worrying about Jackson's men at Harpers Ferry and his own army positioning itself for the defense of South Mountain—he had some relief, leaving Major General Jeb Stuart to guard South Mountain.[35]

Things proved not to be running as smoothly as Hill thought, however. He received no actual orders to defend Turner's Gap, as it appeared there would be no need to do so. Therefore, no troops were left there. Fearing that much of the fighting would occur at Crampton's Gap, General Stuart left two hundred cavalry troops behind at Fox's Gap while he went south to make sure Crampton's Gap was secured. Working as the eyes and ears of the Confederate army, Stuart apparently failed to notify Hill that he needed to post troops at Turner's. On hearing of Union cavalry movements toward South Mountain, Colonel Alfred Colquitt was ordered to deploy. "I was ordered to move at once with my brigade and the battery of artillery. Proceeding along the turnpike 2 or 3 miles, I reached the summit of South Mountain and discovered the enemy's cavalry advancing and ours gradually giving back. I reported my arrival to General Stuart, and consulted with him, as to the best disposition of the forces." After inspecting Colquitt's position, Hill went to make another observation before joining Colquitt and his staff at the Mountain House to eat and to study the current situation.[36]

Brigadier General Samuel Garland was waiting at the Mountain House by the time Hill arrived just behind Colquitt; the news he was about to deliver was not good. The Union army was approaching faster than anyone anticipated. Hill ordered Garland to move his brigade consisting of the 5th, 12th, 13th, 20th and 23rd North Carolina to the south and secure Fox's Gap and hold it at all costs. The ammunition train of the Army of Northern Virginia was at the western base of the mountain, and it would be a devastating blow if it fell into Union hands. Moving a brigade of any size was not easy. The rugged, rocky terrain quickly took its toll on troops who already had marched a long distance carrying heavy equipment. Colonel Duncan K. McRae led the brigade with his 5th North Carolina as quickly as possible in a column of fours. McRae's and the other regiments' movements were shielded by a belt of woods along the eastern flank; however, their movements were slowed by the badly rutted roads.[37]

Garland's brigade moved hastily into position. It moved along the crest of the mountain until the 5th veered east where the Wood Road made a turn west. The 12th North Carolina, commanded by Captain Shugan Snow, and the 23rd, Colonel Daniel H. Christie's men, were moved up and halted on the 5th's left along the ridge road behind a stone wall. General Garland requested McRae accompany him on a reconnaissance.

> *Immediately in front of the ridge road were stubble and corn fields, and, for about 40 paces to the front, a plateau, which suddenly broke on the left into a succession of ravines, and, farther beyond and in front, a ravine, of greater length and depth, extended from the road which ran along the base of the mountain far out into the field, and, connected with the ravine on our left, formed natural parallel approaches to our position.*[38]

The 20th North Carolina went into position just north of the Old Sharpsburg Road behind the stone wall bordering the Wood's Road to the east. On their left, the 13th North Carolina took position along the Wood Road on the eastern slope of the mountain. In front of the 23rd North Carolina, Captain J.W. Bondurant's Alabama battery of four guns took up position. Bondurant's guns were placed close to stone walls to their north and southern flank, leaving the gunners no room to operate. "In spite of the high stone wall on their left flank, the artillerists still managed to get a clear view to their left front."[39]

Early on the morning of September 14, Pleasonton and his cavalry renewed his reconnaissance of the gap and found that the Confederates were already in place in force. He waited and watched the Confederates until help from the infantry arrived. Not long after, two batteries came forward within a short distance of Bolivar and took a position on a knoll about a half mile past the forks of the old Sharpsburg Road and the turnpike, just left of the National Road. They were the 3rd United States Battery C and G under Captain Horatio G. Gibson and the 2nd United States Battery E, led by Lieutenant Samuel N. Benjamin. Once in place, they lobbed shells at Confederate artillery on the mountain[40]

By 6:00 a.m. that same day, Brigadier General Jacob D. Cox marched his division from Middletown toward South Mountain after receiving orders from Major General Jesse L. Reno (Ninth Corps, commanding) to move in support of Brigadier General Alfred Pleasonton's cavalry. Pleasonton had already begun moving up the Hagerstown turnpike, scouting ahead for the Ninth Corps. The division was led by the First Brigade, consisting of the 12th, 23rd and the 30th Ohio Regiments, roughly fifteen hundred troops under the command of Colonel Eliakim P. Scammon. Along with the Ohio regiments was Captain George W. Gilmore's Company L of the 2nd West Virginia Cavalry, Captain William B. Harrison's Company A of the 1st West Virginia Cavalry and Captain James R. McMullin's Ohio Light Artillery. They were to proceed by the Boonsboro Road, just to the left of the Hagerstown turnpike, to see if the Confederates were of considerable force at the crest of South Mountain. The Second Brigade, led by Colonel George Crook, consisted of the 11th, 28th and 36th Ohio Regiments, along with Captain Seth J. Simmonds's battery. Captain Frederick Schambeck's Illinois cavalry troop followed in support.[41]

Not long after their advance started, Colonel Scammon's men heard artillery fire in the distance. It soon became evident that the Confederate army not only held the crest of the mountain but also did so in considerable force. Cox ordered his entire division to engage and remove the enemy from the mountain. Pleasonton's cavalry remained near the mountain, scouting Confederate positions and reporting back to Cox's approaching division. Directing Benjamin and Gibson's batteries, now ready to fully engage the enemy, Pleasonton directed their artillery to lob shells into Turner's Gap, with the hopes of drawing return fire. Not long after, Lane's six guns positioned near the Mountain House returned fire on Union batteries. Although the artillery fire grew rather heated, Union guns had the upper hand and silenced Lane's artillery. It was this heavy artillery fight that Cox's division heard off in the distance as they marched along.

Cox rode to the head of the column to ride along with Scammon. Not long after crossing Catoctin Creek, they encountered Colonel Augustus Moor, who just two days prior had been captured by Wade Hampton's cavalry in the streets of Frederick. Both men were shocked to see Moor; he told Cox and Scammon he had been paroled and was heading back to Union lines. Moor, who was honor bound by his terms of parole, told his friends to be careful, then he turned and walked away. With the rumbling of cannon fire growing louder, Cox rode toward the back of his columns, telling the men to be prepared for what was coming.[42]

As Cox rode back, Scammon's brigade kept marching and met up with Pleasonton on the National Road, about a mile or so beyond the Catoctin. Pleasonton directed Scammon to move his brigade off to the left of the Old Sharpsburg Road, gain the crest of the mountain and then move off to the right of the turnpike and get behind the enemy. Around 7:00 a.m., Scammon turned off the National Road when, shortly after moving beyond Mentzer's Mill, an artillery shell from high up on the mountain showed the position of Confederate troops. Part of the 30th Ohio continued up the mountain by way of the main road until turning off onto a country road near what was once the Reno School House, moving farther to the left and almost parallel to the crest of the mountain. Luckily, the forest shielded their movements from the eyes of the waiting Confederates. The lead regiment was the 23rd Ohio, led by future president of the United States, Lieutenant Colonel Rutherford B. Hayes. His regiment deployed to the left and moved through the woods to the left of the road toward the crest of the mountain to gain, if possible, the Confederate right, "so as to turn it and attack his flank." To the right of the 23rd was the 12th Ohio; on the 12th's right was the 30th Ohio. Soon, the entire line came under fire from the entrenched 5th, 23rd, 20th and 13th, all of North Carolina.[43]

Garland and McRae observed from above the advancement of "persons moving at some distance on the road." Garland ordered fifty skirmishers to halt the Union troops that turned out to be the 23rd Ohio. It was 9:00 a.m. by the time Hayes got moving through the woods to the left of the road; he had one advanced company deployed as skirmishers. Garland ordered McRae to send in support of the 5th North Carolina, and McRae led his entire regiment forward.

> We found the growth very thick, so much so that it was impossible to advance in line of battle. The enemy's skirmishers had advanced almost to the very edge of the woods nearest us, and, as we appeared at the edge, a sharp skirmish fire ensued, with much more effect on our side than on that of the enemy, as we lost no men and several of the enemy were seen to fall and 1 taken prisoner; but at this moment I found that the raw troops on my right, who had never been under fire, had had no drill and had but few officers, were breaking in some confusion, the rest of the line remaining firm.[44]

Hayes had seen McRae charging down the hill on his right and pushed through the thicket as quickly as possible, only to crash head-on into the

5th North Carolina. Soon after the skirmishing began, the remainder of Hayes's regiment was ordered forward. This overwhelming firefight caused the unseasoned men of McRae's regiment to flee the field of battle. Hayes ordered his men to halt and re-form their battle lines. Once this was complete, the fight resumed, and his regiment became so heavily engaged that Hayes had no choice but to order a charge. It was a good call on Hayes's part; it caused the Confederates to turn and run, with the 5th North Carolina falling back to their original position. During this intense fight, the 12th North Carolina advanced close enough to the 23rd Ohio to, along with the 5th North Carolina, fire a musket volley; then both units retreated to their lines in disorder. The 23rd North Carolina during this time was also heading toward the fight from the Wood Road and was about forty yards into an open field, stopping in front of the 23rd Ohio. The 23rd North Carolina volleyed into the 23rd Ohio, damaging the 12th Ohio as well. General Garland ordered the 20th and 13th North Carolina to move in from the left and support the 5th North Carolina.[45]

Although the 12th North Carolina had retreated, the remaining Confederates were still able to put up enough of a fight to halt Hayes's advance. Still very much in the fight, the 23rd Ohio sheltered behind a stone wall at the edge of the woods and poured volley after volley into McRae's men. Colonel T.L. Rosser of the 5th Virginia Cavalry ordered his 250 men to dismount and fire into the 23rd Ohio and then advance toward them. Hayes's men were taking a beating, which was getting worse by the minute. Now Pelham's two guns started firing canister shot from above. Hayes figured that the only way to get out was to make another charge; however, before he could give the order to charge, a bullet struck him above the left elbow, knocking him to the ground. Although severely wounded, he was able to direct the 23rd where he wanted them. When the firing slowed down a bit, Hayes was taken to a surgeon for treatment; Major James Comly assumed command of the 23rd.[46]

On the right of the 23rd Ohio, the 12th Ohio was the center of the brigade line, which moved about a fourth of a mile through heavy pine woods and thickets, only to enter over open ground, drawing heavy fire from the 23rd North Carolina. Finally, it halted to wait for the 30th Ohio on its right to come up and wait for the entire brigade to make a further advance. Seeing it reported to General Garland that "the enemy had massed a very large force in those woods, and were preparing to turn our right," McRae stressed to Garland that his men may be dislodged. He suggested shelling the woods but was informed there was no artillery left, as Bondurant's battery had been hit hard by Ohio sharpshooters and left the line. Garland rode off to the left to check on the progress of the 13th and 20th North Carolina that he had ordered earlier to move forward and support the 5th. He met up with them as they crossed the Old Sharpsburg Road when he saw the commotion from Union skirmishers of the 30th Ohio moving in on his left. From there, he ordered Colonel Alfred Iverson to move his 20th North Carolina to the left of the 23rd North Carolina, still hotly engaged in fighting with Hayes's 23rd Ohio. Iverson did the best he could; the ground was rough, making it difficult to form a line as Garland directed. Instead, Iverson positioned his men along Ridge Road, just to the left and behind the 23rd North Carolina. Once settled into position, he was unable to see much, due to the thick cover of the woods. So, skirmishers were sent forward. The 13th North Carolina at this time was sent in the direction of the Wise Farm.[47]

To the left of the Confederate line, around the same time that the 23rd Ohio forced the 5th North Carolina in the direction of the cornfield on top of the hill, the 13th North Carolina surged forward into Wise's field. In response, the 30th Ohio acted quickly to this movement on its left, moving across the Old Sharpsburg Road into the woods below the North Carolinians and connected with the 12th Ohio in Beachley's field. After entering an open field, the 13th North Carolina's view of what it faced in its front was obstructed by a thick forest. In the forest waited the Ohio skirmishers, who poured a hot, deadly fire into the 13th, forcing them to scatter. It was during this ambush that General Garland turned to give orders to his orderly when a bullet ripped into his chest, killing him. Immediately reacting to Garland's fall from his horse, his staff retrieved him and carried his body back to the Mountain House.[48]

With Garland dead, command passed to McRae, who, upon observing the horrible situation his men were in, reported to D.H. Hill that his forces were too badly damaged to hold out. Shortly after, Colonel C.C. Tew, with the 2nd and 4th North Carolina of General George B. Anderson's brigade, arrived to assist. Tew was about to take a position on the immediate left of the 13th when he received an order from Anderson to move farther to the left. The move left a wide gap in the Confederate line, of which General Hill was quickly notified. McRae ordered the 13th to follow behind Tew to the left and keep close by. McRae then rode off to the right to "move the Fifth North Carolina to the left and fill with it the space vacant in the line, but I found that, under my previous order, this regiment had already been advanced into the field on the right of the Twenty-third, and it was dangerous to withdraw it."[49]

At the same time, the fighting to the south continued. The 12th and 30th Ohio continued inching their way up the hill, seeking whatever cover they could to stay out of the sights of both of the North Carolina regiments in the cornfield to their front left. Union artillery under Captain James McMullin advanced slowly over the rocky terrain and settled in front of the 12th Ohio. It opened fire on the 20th North Carolina, which was hunched down behind a stone wall some four hundred yards away, waiting for the Yankee advance. McMullin's battery was rather exposed, leaving it an easy target for Confederate sharpshooters, who took advantage and picked off members of the Union artillery. After firing off just four rounds, the crews abandoned the artillery, which remained safe from Confederate capture.

Cox gave the order to advance; Scammon sprang quickly into action, with his fourteen hundred men remaining in the brigade. To the left, the 23rd Ohio, led by Major Comly, pushed through a cornfield under fire and smashed into the 23rd North Carolina. Men from both sides melted away with each volley. "Bayonets were freely used, and men on both sides fell under the cutting thrusts." Outnumbered, the North Carolina men finally gave way and abandoned the field. The 23rd Ohio followed, then halted on the mountain crest.[50]

At the same time, on the right of the 23rd Ohio, the 12th charged up the slope with the bayonet, crashing into the 20th North Carolina. The 20th stood firm and fired volley after deadly volley until the Ohio men were just a few feet away, then the 20th retreated over the crest of the mountain into a thicket. The 12th Ohio gave chase until they were about three hundred yards from the crest before Confederate artillery forced them to take cover. After hours of fighting, the scattered retreating Confederates hurried down the western slope of the mountain. As far as the Battle of South Mountain, the fight for Fox's Gap was over for men of the 5th, 20th and 23rd North Carolina.

Lieutenant Colonel Ruffin, commanding the 13th North Carolina, received word after sending his aid to the right to see what was transpiring that the center and right of the brigade was no longer there and Union troops were now on his flank. To his left, the situation did not look much better. Colonel Tew, along with his two regiments from Anderson's brigade, had been ordered to move out. Ruffin then ordered his men to move as well and joined up with the right of Anderson, who now was in command.

It was past noon. While it was evident to General D.H. Hill that he was dealing with a far larger army than they thought, the Confederate general was not ready to give up. The Union army by this time had total control of Fox's Gap; a slight lull in the fighting allowed both sides to rest and resupply

Photograph of Lieutenant General James Longstreet, officer of the Confederate army, taken later in his life. *Library of Congress.*

ammunition. During this time, the Confederate Signal Corps reported to Hill large masses of soldiers in blue near the foot of the mountain. Hill sent an urgent dispatch to General Longstreet. As the smoke from muskets and cannons cleared, Hill realized that not only his current position but also Turner's Gap was in serious trouble. Hill urged Longstreet to hurry. Although Hill was right to be anxious, he did not consider that Cox's men were exhausted from fighting and Colonel G.B. Anderson had a fresh brigade positioned along the Wood Road ready for action.

By the looks of the situation, Hill figured Cox was about to advance all the way to the Mountain House by way of the Wood Road with nothing to oppose him. What Hill failed to realize was that that road was the same occupied by Anderson's brigade. However, Hill ordered two pieces of artillery from the Mountain House to head off the advance of the Ohio men and opened fire on the Ohio skirmishers. The 23rd Ohio, on the left, had already reached the crest by this time and came under heavy cannister fire. On the right, the 30th Ohio also succeeded in reaching the top despite the heavy canister and case shot. To aid Cox's men, McMullin sent a section of his battery forward and opened a hot, accurate fire on the defending Confederates. However, the battery was not in place long after taking heavy fire from Confederate infantry, leaving little choice but to pull back. At this point, Cox decided to wait for reinforcements.[51]

Around 3:30 p.m., Longstreet's lead brigades under Colonel G.T. Anderson and Brigadier General Thomas F. Drayton marched to the Mountain House and reported to Hill. The nineteen hundred men were a welcome sight; Hill felt anxious to neutralize the Union force on his right before the "Yankees made their grand attack," which he felt would be on his left. Hill ordered Anderson, Brigadier General Roswell Ripley and General Drayton to follow a path until they met Rosser's first position, "when they should change their flank, march into the line of battle, and sweep the woods before them." To assist in their movement, Hill ordered a battery to shell the woods in different directions to inflict as much damage as possible. As soon as the brigades were in place, Hill hoped they would make a vigorous attack on the Union soldiers. Before getting into position, however, both Anderson and Drayton were under attack.[52]

Just after 4:00 p.m., Cox had the reinforcements to continue to fight. He then received orders to fully engage while his skirmishers kept Anderson and Drayton in check. Cox ordered the advancement; the awaiting Confederates opened a volley and then charged the Ohio men. The Union numbers were overwhelming, routing the Confederates and forcing them to flee. Brigadier

General Samuel Sturgis moved his second division of the Ninth Corps to the front of Cox's men, occupying the newly gained ground. Although it was starting to get dark, Hill was not done fighting. His Confederates started another attack on the Union's extreme left, but Colonel Harrison Fairchild's 9th, 89th and 103rd New Yorkers quickly repulsed them.[53]

With the sky growing darker by the minute, men on both sides were beyond exhausted. Not ready to give up just yet, the Confederates charged on Sturgis and Cox's Kanawha divisions. The Confederate effort to recapture the lost ground did not last long before the worn-out Confederates pulled back after an hour of fighting. While this was taking place, General Reno rode along his lines, checking to make sure his defense was strong. While he looked at a tree line across the Old Sharpsburg Road, a volley of Confederate muskets fired, hitting Reno in the chest, just under his heart. He slumped forward in his saddle before being helped off his horse by his staff. He died shortly thereafter.

The fighting for Fox's Gap ended when it became too dark to see. "We retreated that night to Sharpsburg, having accomplished all that was required—the delay of the Yankee army until Harper's Ferry could not be relieved," wrote General D.H. Hill. Although a loss for the Confederates, Hill felt pride in what his men had accomplished. He wrote:

> *Should the truth ever be known, the Battle of South Mountain, as far as my division was concerned, will be regarded as one of the most remarkable and creditable of the war. The division had marched all the way from Richmond, and the straggling had been enormous in consequence of heavy marches, deficient commissariat, want of shoes, and inefficient officers. Owing to these combined causes, the division numbered less than 5,000 men the morning of September 14 and had five roads to guard, extending over a space of as many miles. This small force successfully resisted, without support, for eight hours, the whole Yankee army, and, when its supports were beaten; still held the roads, so that our retreat was affected without the loss of a gun, a wagon, or an ambulance.*[54]

TURNER'S GAP

The sun had not even begun to rise on the cool morning of September 14, 1862, when the order came from General Hooker to move out. Anxious to confront the enemy, Hooker wanted no time wasted. Members of the First Corps, including the Iron Brigade, rose quickly and prepared to march on empty stomachs. Within a few short hours, though, the day became hot, and the dry, dusty roads made it difficult to see as the soldiers trudged along the National Road. Marching their way along the Monocacy River, the First Corps passed through Frederick, "a pleasant city," as Private Asahel Gage of the 2nd Wisconsin, Company D wrote in his diary. By 1:00 p.m., the First Corps rested about a mile west of Middletown, along the Catoctin Creek. Hooker, unaware of what lay ahead, rode forward to scout the countryside for a good place to set up for an attack. Off in the distance, he heard the rumbling of cannons.[55]

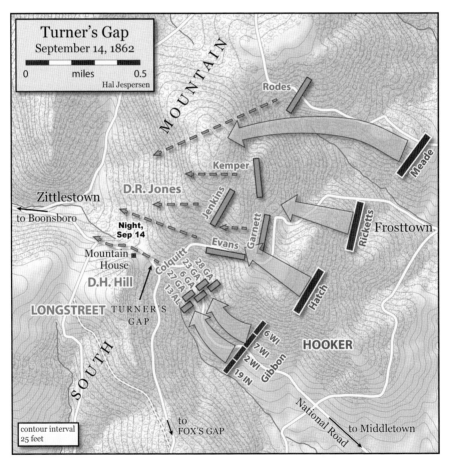

The Union army clashes with the Confederates at Turner's Gap. Map by Hal Jespersen. *www.cwmaps.com.*

From his vantage point, Hooker could see that parts of the Confederate army had already taken possession of Turner's Pass and the crests of the mountain. To the north of the pass, General Longstreet dug in, prepared to fight. To his right was Brigadier General D.R. Jones, of Jones's division. Ensconced in a deep drainage on the north side of the National Road, blocking the pass, stood Colonel Alfred H. Colquitt with his brigade, all prepared to fight. Hooker continued his reconnaissance of the eastern slope, which extended far north and south of the National Road. The slopes of South Mountain were wooded and rugged, making it difficult for any army to ascend. The National Road runs northwest and southeast, crossing the summit of the mountain through a deep gorge.[56]

Around 2:00 p.m., with his scouting about complete, Hooker ordered General George Meade to move his division to the right of the National Road. This would serve as a "diversion" to allow General Reno's Ninth Corps to move south of the road. Generals John Porter Hatch and James Ricketts were ordered to follow Meade in support. The three divisions moved into position by way of the Hagerstown Road to the vicinity of Mount Tabor Church and made a turn to the west into open fields. By 4:00 p.m. the divisions were moving toward the Confederate position, with Meade on the right, Hatch to the left and Ricketts in reserve.[57]

The awaiting Confederates saw every move the Union soldiers made and opened fire from one of their batteries higher up on the mountainside. Not wasting any time, Union guns answered back from Captain James Cooper's Battery B of the 1st Pennsylvania Light Artillery. The 13th Pennsylvania Reserves (Bucktails) Infantry was deployed as skirmishers following the artillery blasts from Copper's battery. They were met with strong resistance from the 6th Alabama of Brigadier General Robert E. Rodes's brigade. Colonel John B. Gordon, the commander of the 6th Alabama, poured a hot, steady fire into the oncoming Pennsylvania Bucktails, followed by a charge that drove them back a short distance. However, the

General George Meade. *Library of Congress.*

49

Bucktails soon had assistance from the 1ˢᵗ and 2ⁿᵈ Pennsylvania Infantries. Satisfied with his observations that the Confederates were well dug in, Hooker ordered Meade to extend his division farther to the right and outflank the Confederate left. Hatch and Ricketts followed Meade's movement to the right as well.

With the far right of the division in place, about a mile and a half from the National Road, Seymour's brigade was the farthest north. On his left flank was Colonel Thomas F. Gallagher's' Third Brigade, and to his left was Colonel Albert L. Magilton's Second Brigade. Now all in place, Hooker ordered Meade to advance his division toward the Confederates, who were protected by rocks, trees and stone fences that lined the fields. To Meade's front, the hills grew larger with each step and the slopes on the eastern side became more rugged, making it difficult to move at a fast pace.

General Rodes's brigade consisted of the 3ʳᵈ, 5ᵗʰ, 6ᵗʰ, 12ᵗʰ and 26ᵗʰ Alabama, and from their position they observed Meade's division approaching at a slow pace. Confederate skirmishers were sent forward and to the left to slow down the Pennsylvanians even more. Lieutenant Robert E. Park of the 12ᵗʰ Alabama took forty men to the foot of the mountain and opened fire. Hooker was cautious in making his plan of attack; it was almost 5:00 p.m. by the time Meade was ordered to advance.[58]

Park's skirmishers were well concealed behind rocks, trees and bushes. The remainder of Meade's division pushed through the woods; before long, they were within easy range of Park's skirmishers, and more shooting occurred. Those who did not fall quickly reorganized the line and pressed forward. Taking whatever cover they could find, the Union soldiers were able to steady themselves and take aim. A steady flow of musket fire kept Mead's men in check, but that would soon change. Park could see more men in blue approaching. It would be a matter of time before he and his skirmishers would be overrun. He ordered his men to retreat but to continue shooting as they did so. Seeing one of his men badly injured, Park ran to his aid. But there was nothing that could be done, and the Confederate lieutenant soon found himself a Yankee prisoner.[59]

There was not much doubt in General Rodes's mind after seeing Park's skirmish line retreat that his men would not be able to hold out if he did not shift his defensive line. "The only chance to continue the fight was to change my front so as to face to the left," Rodes wrote in his battle report. He gave the order for all his regiments to retreat up the gorge and sides of the mountain and to continue fighting as they moved. This move allowed Rodes to maintain the higher ground and "face the enemy's right again." The 6ᵗʰ Alabama was ordered to move farther to the north and hold the higher ground. The 5th was ordered to move to the left and take the 6th's old position and dig in.[60]

Seeing that the higher ground to the north was open, General Truman Seymour advanced in that direction, knowing the heights would allow him to strain the defending Confederates. However, the 6th Alabama beat them to the "prominent hill." A brisk volley of Confederate musket and artillery fire opened on Seymour's brigade from the upper left of the mountain. Seymour's Pennsylvanians had a difficult task ahead of them, and with casualties mounting rapidly, action needed to be taken—and fast!

Now that all of Meade's division was advancing forward, Colonel Joseph W. Fisher, with his 5th Pennsylvania Reserves, poured a heavy, devastating fire into the 6th Alabama. Colonel John B. Gordon held out as long as he could. With the constant advancing of Meade's division, the Rebel colonel could see that his time was limited. In order to prevent unnecessary loss, Gordon was left with little choice; retreat was the only option. "Gordon's regiment retired slowly, now being under an enfilading as well as direct fire and in danger of being surrounded, but was still, fortunately for the whole command, held together by its able commander," Rodes wrote. Gordon's men moved as fast as they could up the mountain, with Seymour's men following. After gaining possession of the north spur at the summit, the Confederate left had been successfully turned.[61]

With many Confederate prisoners taken, Seymour's brigade was sent to the rear. Their fate was yet to be determined. From his position on the high ground, Seymour could see a cornfield as well as a stone wall lined with Confederate troops. This would have been the left wing of the 5th Alabama. They wasted no time in firing on Seymour and his division. The Pennsylvanians answered back with a volley of their own and leveled their rifles, their bayonets already fixed. With three loud cheers, the Pennsylvanians set off at a fast pace and drove the 5th Alabamians up the mountain.[62]

The Confederate left had been turned. Rodes could see how bad things were going and knew it would not be long before Seymour's men broke his left flank and got behind his line. Although only Seymour's brigade has been mentioned so far, his was not the only one of Meade's division to step forward when ordered. Seymour's brigade was able to move faster, as the terrain was not the same throughout the South Mountain. Therefore, not all of Meade's division was engaged at the same time. While Seymour's brigade was attacking Rodes's left, the brigades of Gallagher and Magilton had also moved forward, heading toward the 5th, 3rd, 26th and 12th Alabama.

Gallagher, along with Magilton's brigades, charged through a gorge to where the 26th and 3rd Alabama were dug in along with part of the right wing of the 5th Alabama. Both brigades moved as quickly as possible over rocky terrain. The well-concealed Confederates continued pouring a hot masking fire of not only artillery but also musketry into them. From their locations, the soldiers of Gallagher's and Magilton's brigades could not see, except for Confederate skirmishers, anyone else shooting at them. Gallagher's brigade continued forward, making progress little by little through the gorge. They were met by a deadly fire from the 3rd and 12th Alabama. Diving for cover, the 11th Pennsylvanians took a heavy loss but returned fire.

To their right was the 9th Pennsylvania Reserves approaching the Haupt Farm, which a group of skirmishers from the 3rd Alabama used as cover. As the 9th neared the farm buildings, the 3rd opened a deadly fire, putting the 9th at a standstill. Lieutenant Colonel Robert Anderson's regiment took immediate shelter behind a stone wall and returned fire. Colonel Gallagher was shot in the arm by a musket ball as he directed his men to cover and was forced to leave the battlefield. Command of the Third Brigade was handed over to Anderson, who now directed his men to put all their firepower onto the farmhouse. Captain Richard Gustin's 12th Reserves, on the left of the brigade, was soon under fire as they eased their way into position on the 11th's left. However, Gustin's reserves were able to continue forward to the woods at the foot of the hill. The 9th and 11th Pennsylvania were still under heavy fire and unable to dislodge the well-covered Alabamians.[63]

Seeing the 9th Pennsylvania pinned down, Meade ordered Lieutenant Colonel Adoniram J. Warner of the 10th Pennsylvania Reserves to assist. Earlier in the battle, Meade had shifted Warner's reserves to reinforce Seymour's First Brigade, but it turned out they were not needed. Following Meade's orders, Warner hurried to the 9th's aid, coming under heavy fire as they neared their position. Warner's reserves settled to the right of the 9th, the additional firepower from the 10th eased the pressure on both the 9th and 11th Pennsylvania and helped them break the stalemate. Under heavy fire, the 3rd Alabama was no longer able to hold out and began their retreat up the mountain. General Rodes described his movements as follows:

In the first attack of the enemy up the bottom of the gorge, they pushed on so vigorously as to catch Captain Ready and a portion of his party of skirmishers, and to separate the Third from the Fifth Alabama Regiment. The Third made a most gallant resistance at this point and had my line been a continuous one it could never have been forced. Having re-established my line, though still with wide intervals, necessarily, on the high peak (this was done under constant fire and in full view of the enemy, now in full possession of the extreme left hill and of the gorge), the fight at close quarters was resumed, and again accompanied by the enemy throwing their, by this time apparently interminable right around toward my rear. In this position, the Sixth Alabama and the Twelfth suffered pretty severely. The latter, together with the remainder of the Third Alabama, which had been well handled by Colonel [C.A.] Battle, was forced to retire, and in so doing lost heavily.[64]

Anderson ordered his men to charge the farmhouse, capturing several prisoners and pursing the rest of the 3rd Alabama until they reached the mountain summit. The charge came to a halt when Anderson's men ran out of ammunition, although, luckily for them, help came at dark. Brigadier General Abram Duryee with his First Brigade of the Second Division from the First Corps came to Anderson's aid. Duryee's brigade consisted of 97th, 104th, 105th New York and the 107th Pennsylvania, led by Captain James M. Thomson. Duryee's brigade held their position while Anderson's brigade withdrew to resupply their ammunition and remained there the rest of the night. They all fought hard. Anderson wrote, "Every officer and man of this command did his duty nobly."[65]

With Gallagher's and Seymour's brigades fighting their way up the hill against Rodes, Colonel Magilton's Second Brigade hammered Confederate brigadier general Nathan G. Evans's small South Carolina brigade with a strong blow. Magilton moved forward with his 8th, 7th and 4th Reserves in line (left to right) and entered the same difficult terrain that gave the other regiments trouble. Magilton detached the 3rd Pennsylvania Reserves to "watch the road we had just come out."[66] With fewer obstacles in the way, the 8th and 7th reached the Confederate line first and poured a deadly fire into F.W. McMaster's 17th South Carolina. "Colonel Stevens soon became engaged with a much superior force, two columns of the enemy advancing rapidly upon his small command," wrote General Evans.[67] Stevens had not been in his assigned position long and hardly settled when Magilton attacked. Stevens, with his Holcombe Legion, had sent out skirmishers minutes before, and they encountered the 8th Pennsylvania Reserves, who found their way into a peach orchard. Stevens's skirmishers had no trouble pushing the 8th Pennsylvania back until the rest of the regiment caught up. Retreating to their line of defenses, the skirmishers passed by the 17th, who were taking aim at the oncoming men in blue.

Now that Stevens's right flank was actively engaged with the 8th, the 4th and 7th Reserves struck Stevens's center. To the left of the 17th South Carolina was the 18th, under Colonel W.H. Wallace; to their left was Lieutenant Colonel T.C. Watkins's 22nd and the 23rd led by Captain S.A. Durham, the left flank of Stevens's South Carolina Brigade. Durham's 23rd made a short advancement forward until meeting up with the skirmishers from the Holcombe Legion and retreated as large numbers of Union soldiers came at them. When the skirmishers were safely behind their lines, Durham ordered his men to open fire on the charging Yankees. The outnumbered South Carolina brigade fought hard but could not hold the Yankees off. In the distance, Durham could see what was probably the 12th Pennsylvania Reserves advancing toward them. He gave the order to withdraw up the mountain. The 22nd South Carolina continued to fight for several more minutes, but with the 23rd on the left leaving their position, Watkins had little choice but to also fall back. As he rallied his men, Watkins was shot dead by a Union bullet, throwing the retreating 22nd into more confusion.[68]

Before the heavy fighting started, the 18th's Colonel W.H. Wallace was ordered to assist General Rodes's brigade, which was at this time retreating. Unable to help Rodes, Stevens commanded Wallace to "change front forward on first company and advance." The plan was to attack the enemy flank; Wallace did so and became fully engaged in combat with the 4th Reserves. Shortly after, Wallace noticed a "heavy column of enemy appearing upon our left flank." The heavy column was more than likely the 12th Reserves and other enemy soldiers forcing Rodes's men back and threatening to get behind Wallace. Although under fire, Wallace fired back on the advancing Yankee soldiers but could not hang on for long. Wallace ordered his men to retreat; facing back toward the mountain, they slowly made their way to the top and positioned on the right of the 22nd South Carolina.[69]

It would not be long until the 17th South Carolina had to give way, as well. They fought hard against the attacking Union soldiers, but between the other regiments retreating and the heavy loss of troops, the 17th had no choice but to retreat, as well. The Carolina troops retreated about three hundred yards, but that would not last long. They were on the verge of being flanked again by hard-fighting Union troops. The 17th had no other choice but to retreat again. McMaster was ordered to form his men on the left of the Jenkins's brigade; however, it became too dark. Left with no options, Evans ordered him to fall back to the National Road.[70]

With their fight over, Meade's men were exhausted, hungry and in need of ammunition. As darkness came, the men filled their cartridge boxes and cared for their wounded comrades. It had been a hard, exhausting fight over difficult terrain, and rest was needed. Hooker seemed pleased with his men; Meade offered further praise of his hard-fighting division. Meade would not be the only division commander to be proud of the work his men did. That same day, General John P. Hatch's division was also victorious.

As Meade's man launched their frontal attack against Rode's Alabamians, Hatch's men began their march into battle. It was 5:00 p.m. by the time the attack started, with daylight fading fast. Hatch was ordered to strike at his front and carry the south spur of Turner's Gap while Meade carried the north. Hatch had four brigades under his command; the biggest, led by General Gibbon, was under Major General Ambrose E. Burnside's order at Bolivar to advance up the National Pike to meet Alfred Colquitt head-on. His other three brigades settled in on Meade's left and marched north along the Mount Tabor Road until they reached their assigned position. When the three brigades began their advance, they formed into three lines of battle: Brigadier General Marsena Patrick's brigade was in front, followed by Hatch's own brigade (led now by Colonel Walther Phelps Jr.); Brigadier General Abner Doubleday's brigade followed in the rear.

General Patrick's Third Brigade consisted of the 21st New York, led by Colonel William F. Rogers, 23rd New York led by Colonel Henry C. Hoffman, 35th New York led by Colonel Newton B. Lord and the 80th New York (20th Militia) led by Lieutenant Colonel Theodore B. Gates. Rifle fire from the entrenched Confederates caused the Union advance to start slow. Patrick ordered the 21st and 35th New York to move forward as skirmishers. Colonel Rogers with the 21st, on the far right of the advancing line, went first with orders to move up a ravine. The 35th was positioned to the south of the 21st, forming the left of the Union line. These two regiments were the entire front of the division, with the rest of Patrick's brigade, the 23rd New York and the 80th New York, behind in support of the skirmishers.[71]

Confederate brigadier general James Kemper arrived with his small brigade, consisting of the 1st, 7th, 11th, 17th and 24th Virginia, at Turner's Gap around 5:00 p.m., consisting of about four hundred men. They were exhausted after a long day marching down dusty roads. Not far behind came Brigadier General Richard B. Garnett's brigade of Virginians (8th, 18th, 19th, 28th and 56th), followed by Colonel Joseph Walker's brigade of South Carolinians (1st, 2nd Rifles, 5th, 6th, 4th South Carolina Battalion and Palmetto Sharpshooters). These brigades were part of the division of D.R. Jones's division, Longstreet's command.

Major General Abner Doubleday of General Staff U.S. Volunteers Infantry Regiment, in uniform, with his wife, Mary Hewitt Doubleday. *Library of Congress*.

The roaring gunfire from D.H. Hill's division alarmed Longstreet, whose men were ascending the western side of the mountain. He hurried his exhausted men under the commands of Kemper, Garnett and Jenkins up the National Pike past the Mountain House where it turned northeasterly along the Dahlgren Road. The brigade commanders did as commanded and soon came under fire of Captain George Durell's Ninth Corp's battery, which was positioned near the Old Sharpsburg Road. The Union battery pounded the Virginians as they moved into position. A spent artillery shell that failed to explode hit Private John H. Daniel of the 1st Virginia on the rear end, throwing him about ten feet. Strangely, he was not seriously harmed.[72]

Kemper's brigade led the way, followed by Garnett with Jenkins in support. Kemper placed his men near the summit of the south spur, facing northeasterly. From their position, Kemper's brigade could hear the fighting of Magilton's Pennsylvanians and Rodes's Alabamians. Garnett's brigade followed with the 56th Virginia anchoring the left of Garnett's line, not far from Kemper's 17th Virginia. Garnett's right, the 8th Virginia, rested in a thick patch of woods. His left, the 56th Virginia, was positioned in a field of standing corn. Once settled, skirmishers were sent forward "to ascertain the position of the enemy."[73]

A short time before sunset, Garnett received an order from General D.R. Jones to detach his left regiment (56th Virginia) and send it about two hundred yards farther to the left and aid Kemper's right. The rest of Garnett's command was to withdraw to a wooded ridge to the rear. The 56th Virginia had barely begun to move out, leaving the 28th Virginia as Garnett's anchor, when Union skirmishers under Hatch's division showed up, followed by the main body. Marsena Patrick led Hatch's advance. The 21st New York on his far right and the 35th forming the left of the line advanced toward Garnett's skirmishers. Confusion set in with the advancing Union lines as a wide gap developed in the skirmish line. The 21st New York went too far to the right while the 35th New York moved too far left, heading toward the National Road. Patrick rode forward to reconnect his skirmish line, but, in the process, he came under fire from Garnett's Virginians.[74]

Patrick ordered the 23rd and 80th New York regiments forward, as well. The 80th was to move forward until connecting with the left wing of the 21st. Likewise, the 23rd was to advance forward until forming the right of the 35th New York. Frustrated by how slow his division was advancing, General Hatch himself rode forward to see what the holdup was. Catching up with Phelps, Hatch ordered him to send forward his skirmishers. Luckily for Phelps, the ground to his front facilitated maneuvering and allowed his men to advance unobserved. "The line of skirmishers, steadily moving forward, at length drew a scattering fire from the enemy, and perceiving that the distance to their position was but about 80 paces, I ordered the brigade to advance in line of battle," Phelps wrote. Garnett's skirmishers fired several volleys into the advancing Union lines and then quickly backed up to their main line behind a stone fence. Phelps's men returned fire, then pursued a short distance before they were in range of Garnett's main line. A hot, deadly volley poured into the charging Union soldiers. Phelps's men ducked behind any cover they could find and returned fire.

With Phelps's men making the attack uphill, Phelps found they were in a bad position and needed to move. Hatch rode through the line cheering on his men, but despite his encouragement, Phelps's men would have to move—and quick. Phelps ordered a charge; many of his men dropped to the ground either killed or wounded, but most were able to return fire that hit their marks with deadly accuracy. As Phelps's brigade moved forward, Hatch continued riding through the lines, yelling words of encouragement. After several minutes of continuous fire from both sides, Garnett's line began to yield. The 28th Virginia, on his left, gave way and fell back to Kemper's right, and the 8th Virginia, on the right of Garnett's line, also gave way and formed along Jenkins's brigade, which was coming to aid Garnett. The Confederate line retreated some two hundred yards, leaving many wounded men where they lay. Colonel John B. Strange of the 19th Virginia was killed, while General Hatch was shot. General Abner Doubleday took over Hatch's command.[75]

Just as Phelps's charge started, Patrick's 35th and 23rd New York arrived to aid in the charge. The large number of men in blue spooked the 8th and 18th Virginia. The fighting did not end with Garnett's withdrawal. As darkness fell, the two sides continued exchanging shots at each other. Patrick's and Phelps's men were relieved just after dark by Abner Doubleday's former brigade of nearly one thousand men. They exchanged shots with the remaining Confederates throughout the night.

The remaining men of Garnett's, Walker's and Kemper's brigades fell back toward the Mountain House, where they met up with other survivors from Rodes's and Stevens's brigades. These men put up a strong, deadly fight against Meade and Hatch but could not prevent them from gaining the high ground. Although the fighting resulted in a high number of casualties for Meade and Hatch, John Gibbon's Fourth Brigade suffered the worst.

While the fighting to the north of the National Road was in progress, General Gibbon had his hands full on the National Road itself. Following Burnside's orders to attack the Confederate center up the main pike, Gibbon's

Portrait of Brigadier General John Gibbon, officer of the Federal army (major general from June 7, 1864). *Library of Congress.*

brigade—consisting of the 19th Indiana, 2nd Wisconsin, 7th Wisconsin and 6th Wisconsin—was detached from the First Corps for the "purpose of making a demonstration." Gibbon's opponent, who was waiting ahead in the gorge, was Colonel Alfred H. Colquitt with his brigade from D.H. Hill's division. The well-protected Colquitt had been in place for several hours waiting for any flanking maneuver the Union's First Corps might try.

Just west of Bolivar, Gibbon ordered his men to a halt to give time for Meade and Hatch to begin their assaults. With the downtime, Gibbon's men relaxed. Some wrote letters to their loved ones, others slept and some, like Private Asahel Gage of Company D, 2nd Wisconsin, boiled water for coffee. The respite did not last for long, however, before Gibbon's men came under direct Confederate artillery fire. A shell struck Gage in the head, killing him and three other soldiers instantly. "I could not see that he made a move," wrote Sergeant Alexander F. Lee of the 2nd Wisconsin.[76]

Around 5:00 p.m., the order for Gibbon to advance came, and the Iron Brigade went into formation. Establishing his brigade on both sides of the road, Gibbon placed the 7th Wisconsin, led by Captain John Callis, to the right of the road. Colonel Edward Bragg's 6th Wisconsin was to the 7th's right and slightly behind. To the right of the 19th Indiana, the 2nd Wisconsin was positioned, led by Colonel Lucius Fairchild. Colonel Solomon Meredith's

19th Indiana was placed on the left side, with Captain William W. Dudley's Company B from the 19th moving farther to the left as flankers. The brigades pressed forward, with companies from the 2nd and 6th Wisconsin ordered forward as skirmishers under the command of Captain Wilson Colwell.

About seven hundred yards from the Mountain House, Colonel Colquitt's brigade was ready to fight. The brigade had been in place anxiously listening to all the fighting around them; now, it was their turn. The 23rd Georgia under Colonel William P. Barclay and the 28th Georgia under Maj Tully Graybill stood on the north side of the National Road. The 28th Georgia, behind a stone fence and woods, anchored Colquitt's far left. To their right sat the 23rd, which took cover behind the same stone wall with their right in a shallow ravine. Hidden by cover, the 23rd was in the best shape, as they would be out of sight until Gibbon's men came within forty yards or so from their position. South of the road, making up the right of Colquitt's line, was the 6th Georgia, 27th Georgia and, anchoring the right, the 13th Alabama. With the Confederates protected by a stone fence, thick woods and a ravine, Gibbon's men would be in for a tough fight.

Now that Gibbon's men were advancing, Colquitt sent skirmishers out in force. From the left of his line, two companies from the 23rd and 28th Georgia went forward. On the right of his line, south of the road, another four companies advanced in front of Colquitt's main line. After moving several hundred yards forward, the men took shelter behind stone walls, thick trees, large boulders and even the home of D. Beachley. There, these men waited for Gibbon's advance.

Not long after the skirmishers from the 2nd and 6th Wisconsin began their advance, they met with enemy fire. Both the 2nd and 6th were roughly one hundred yards in front of the main regiment bodies. The 7th Wisconsin, on the right of the line, was supported by the 6th; to the left, the 19th Indiana was supported by the 2nd Wisconsin, about two hundred yards roughly to their rear. "The enemy had a battery placed well up in the gorge, which immediately opened upon us," Gibbon wrote. Although under heavy fire, the Union skirmishers and supporting regiments continued advancing and firing as often as they could. Both the 7th Wisconsin and 19th Indiana soon caught up to the skirmishers and took part in the gunfight. All the while, Union artillery under Lieutenant James Stewart continued moving up the road until they were within range of Colquitt's position. The 19th Indiana was advancing on the left of the road, albeit slowly due to Confederate fire from the Beachley house and woods. Stewart's guns opened fire on those stubborn Georgians and silenced their fire, although temporarily, until they reached new cover deeper in the woods. The Georgians then reopened fire, halting the 19th Indiana until its colonel ordered the regiment forward to fight at close quarters. Not long after, the Georgians yielded, and the 19th Indiana followed with the 2nd Wisconsin on its right.[77]

Colonel Lucius Fairchild ordered his regiment forward, creeping along under fire from Confederate sharpshooters. The 2nd moved more to the right of the Indiana, closer to the turnpike and filling the gap between them and the 19th. After firing twenty rounds of ammunition, the incoming rounds from Confederate lines ceased. "Then I ordered the men to fire by the right-oblique, on a line of the enemy who was firing on the 7th Wisconsin," wrote Fairchild. Shortly after, Fairchild ordered a ceasefire to let the smoke clear and get a better look. After it cleared, he ordered skirmishers from Company A deployed to the left of the 19th Indiana in order to prevent a surprise attack from the Confederates. More firing from hidden Confederates melted away the Union skirmish lines; shots seemed to have come from every direction. As the firing grew more intense, men dropped fast, including Captain Wilson Colwell, a former mayor of La Crosse. "His place can hardly be filled," wrote Fairchild."[78]

On the far right of the line, the 6th Wisconsin continued advancing behind the 7th, about one hundred yards behind the two companies of skirmishers the 6th had sent earlier. They had been marching through a cornfield for a half mile or so before coming out into a wide-open field. Confederate skirmishers from the 23rd Georgia were behind a stone fence and poured a deadly fire into Union skirmishers, making the advance difficult. Callis's 7th Wisconsin regiment quickly formed a line of battle, its left anchored on the National Road and its right near a woodlot on the southern slope of the mountain. The 23rd Georgia continued firing, causing severe damage among Union ranks with no protection in the open field. Answering the 23rd's fire, the 7th Wisconsin responded as quickly and as deadly as possible before advancing again. However, they did not move far before another round of deadly fire, this time from the woods on its right and from above the stone fence toward the crest of the mountain, drastically thinned the 7th's ranks. Luckily for Callis and his men, the 6th Wisconsin was quickly advancing roughly fifty yards behind at this point.[79]

Shots rang out at the 6th's skirmishers not long after advancing. They had found Colquitt's men sooner than expected. The gunfire grew more intense with every passing second, and soon the 7th Wisconsin was there to render aid to the 6th's skirmishers. Although the 7th Wisconsin helped take some pressure off, soon, the 7th needed help themselves. Not only seeing, but also hearing the intense fighting ahead, Lieutenant Colonel Bragg deployed the 6th quickly, with his right flank opening fire as soon as they could, smashing into the 23rd and 28th Georgia.

"I also moved the left wing by the right flank into the rear of the right wing, and commenced a fire by the wings alternately, and advancing the line after each volley," Bragg wrote. With the light of day pretty much gone and the ground steep and full of rocks making it rather difficult to maneuver, Bragg did the best he could on receiving an order from Gibbon to flank Colquitt's left. Without hesitation, the 6th Wisconsin moved swiftly in the dark and formed a new battle line. Now the left of the 6th covered the 7th Wisconsin, and its right flank extended into an open field. Dawes gave the order for his men prone. As the men did this, the right wing passed over the left wing and fired a round of shot into the woods. Then they went to the ground, and the left wing repeated the action. This action happened two more times, with the 7th Wisconsin cheering on their fellow soldiers.[80]

While the 6th and 7th Wisconsin had been able to advance faster than the 19th Indiana and the 2nd Wisconsin, they suffered far more in the end. Meanwhile, the 2nd Wisconsin and 19th Indiana had made progress on the left by dislodging the Confederates to their front. Both regiments were able to overpower the 13th Alabama, 27th Georgia and 6th Georgia and herd them west toward the tree-lined hillside below the Mountain House. Once stopped, the 2nd Wisconsin could see the struggles of the 7th Wisconsin and poured their oblique fire toward the 23rd Georgia, although little damage was done to the 23rd due to the cover of the stone fence. The 2nd Wisconsin was able to keep up the firing for roughly ten minutes until their ammunition ran low and it was too dark to see. They fixed bayonets, along with the 19th Indiana, and held the gained ground until relieved. They badly needed some rest. "I could write a volume of what I have seen," wrote Private William P. Taylor of the 2nd Wisconsin after the Battle of South Mountain. Luckily for the 6th and 7th Wisconsin, the Confederate skirmish line disappeared into the night, retreating to their main line of defense up the mountain.[81]

The Iron Brigade had fought hard, advancing under heavy enemy fire and firing their weapons until they were almost too hot to fire. Surrounding the Iron Brigade, other parts of the Army of the Potomac had been successful. Unfortunately, the midwesterners could not bask in the same glory. They fought hard but lost badly. Acting brigade surgeon Dr. A.J. Ward said, "Our regiments have suffered severely, but they have the proud satisfaction of knowing that in every battle they have fought manfully, driven the rebels and held the ground."[82]

4

ON TO ANTIETAM CREEK

Early the next morning, September 15, civilians could not wait to rush reports to McClellan about the Confederates' disorganized mass retreat. When it was known for sure that Lee had retreated, McClellan ordered his cavalry to move out in advance of Hooker's, Sumner's and Mansfield's corps. McClellan issued orders to pursue Lee immediately and crush his army. Burnside and Porter marched along the Old Sharpsburg Road. Franklin, with his corps, was to advance into Pleasant Valley and halt at Rohrersville with the possibility of relieving Harpers Ferry. However, Franklin soon learned that help was no longer needed at Harpers Ferry and continued to Sharpsburg.

The pursuit of Lee down South Mountain was difficult for all involved. Not even a full twenty-four hours had passed since the heated exchange at all three gaps, with the men still exhausted. The Iron Brigade, known for their hard fighting, along with their black hats, was no different. Sergeant William H. Harries of Company B, 2nd Wisconsin, recalled when marching "finding myself going to sleep as I walked, my gun dropping out of my hand." After the loss at Second Bull Run, followed by the hectic fight at Turner's Gap, the Wisconsin regiments had shrunk considerably since their organization. That, however, would not demoralize the Iron Brigade, and they did not lack courage. Although tired and having a difficult time marching down "rough roads," the Wisconsin men, with the rest of the First Corps, marched on.[83]

When night fell on September 14, General Lee realized the fight at South Mountain had gone against him and abandoned his northern invasion plan for the time being. Lee soon sent dispatches to Jackson to march from Harpers

Ferry to cover the main army crossing the Potomac at Shepherdstown Ford. Longstreet and D.H. Hill were to push their commands to Hagerstown. The retreat harshly affected Longstreet's command; the large numbers of stragglers demoralized the remaining soldiers, making the march harder. By early morning on the fifteenth, Longstreet's command was crossing the Antietam Creek with General D.H. Hill's division. They took place in a line of battle between the Antietam and the village of Sharpsburg. Not long after getting into position, Longstreet received word that Harpers Ferry was in control of Jackson's men.

As Lee's army continued advancing toward Sharpsburg, Union Cavalry chief major general Alfred Pleasonton, with the 8th Illinois Cavalry, led by Colonel John F. Farnsworth, continued ahead of the main army. Pleasonton's cavalry neared Boonsboro before clashing with the 4th and 9th Virginia Cavalry. Farnsworth led the Union charge; Fitzhugh Lee led the Confederate. Lee's cavalry checked the charging Union cavalry, forcing them to back off. Unlike the Union cavalry, Lee's troopers had been in the saddle for the previous four days before finally being able to dismount. Their rest was short-lived, as Pleasonton and Farnsworth made their appearance. It was a rather short fight that resulted in the Confederate cavalry continuing to push through Boonsboro.

Major General Israel B. Richardson's division, of the Union's Second Corps, was able to pass through Boonsboro, then on to Keedysville before finding the tail end of the Confederate army. By this time, Longstreet and Hill had already positioned themselves across Antietam Creek. Richardson ordered a messenger sent to McClellan notifying him of enemy strength and position. On hearing the reports, McClellan directed all corps, except for Franklin's, to get to Sharpsburg quickly. McClellan had hoped to give battle to Lee's distraught army on September 15. However, his forces had not moved quickly enough. His instructions were to attack Lee if on the march but not to engage if positioned in force until receiving further orders. McClellan wrote:

> On arriving at the front in the afternoon, I found but two divisions. Richardson's and Sykes' in position. The rest were halted in the road, the head of the column some distance in rear of Richardson. After a rapid examination of the position, I found that it was too late to attack that day, and at once directed locations to be selected for our batteries of position, and indicated the bivouacs for the different corps, massing them near and on both sides of the Sharpsburg Pike.[84]

Portrait of Brigadier General Israel B. Richardson, officer of the Federal army (major general from July 4, 1862). *Library of Congress.*

The Wisconsin Iron Brigade, with the rest of the First Corps, marched on September 15 through Boonsboro, then veered to the left and followed the road toward Sharpsburg. Along the way, the First Corps found several small bridges burned by the retreating Confederates. For several miles, there were many bridges still smoking, and before long, the First Corps reached the banks of the Antietam. From their location, members of the Iron Brigade could see the Confederate position.[85]

Hooker received orders from McClellan to bivouac for the night after crossing a small stone bridge where the Little and Big Antietam Creeks meet. Meanwhile, the divisions of Brigadier General William H. French and Major General John Sedgwick, of the Second Corps, arrived at Sharpsburg, going into position to the rear of Richardson and on either side of the Sharpsburg turnpike. Sedgwick was to the right, with French on the left. General Mansfield's Twelfth Corps remained in place at Nicodemus Mills until the next day. General Burnside was ordered to move farther to the left of the main army.[86]

During the night, many soldiers took advantage of the downtime to sleep, while others took to pen and paper, writing home to their families—possibly for the last time. Eighteen-year-old Private Franklin Gerlaugh and nineteen-year-old Private William P. Black, both of Company A, 6th Wisconsin, enjoyed a much-needed rest. Franklin and Black had been best friends for years; both were from Fredonia, Wisconsin, and had joined on May 10, 1861.

Sergeant John B. David of Company E, 2nd Wisconsin, used the evening to start a letter to a fallen comrade's father. The comrade had died at South Mountain. David was born in Illinois and worked as a farmer until moving to Oshkosh, Wisconsin, in time to enlist on April 20, 1861. During the Battles of South Mountain and Antietam, David held the rank of corporal. He was promoted to sergeant on December 16, 1862. Although he survived the war, he was captured at Gettysburg on July 1, 1863, and remained a prisoner of war until February 2, 1865.

Private Elon Brown of Company H, 2nd Wisconsin, wrote to his family, updating them on what had happened since his last letter. Brown, who "had a good many close calls" at South Mountain, was born in 1839 in New York, the third-oldest child of James and Malvina Brown. He had three brothers and four sisters. When Elon was young, his father moved the family to Jefferson, Wisconsin, for reasons unknown. He enlisted in the army on May 19, 1861, and would serve until his discharge date in June 1864. He left Wisconsin for New Hampshire, where he taught at a university until his death on August 19, 1869.

Private William P. Taylor of Company E, 2nd Wisconsin, wrote until darkness stopped him. Like many other soldiers, Taylor wanted his family to know he was still "among the living." Although his writing was cut short due to the sun dropping off into the horizon, Taylor was able to speak of the horrors of South Mountain. He wrote the following: "It was not my intention, sir, to write you a lengthy letter. As indeed, I have not time. I am devoting this day to writing letters for the men who are dying, and those who are severely wounded and who requested me to do so. All who are remaining were first rate, ready for anything."

For those who were not already up at dawn on the morning of September 16, the sounds of artillery woke them. The exchange of artillery fire took place all day, with little to no damage caused to either side. McClellan and his staff rode from one high point to another using his field glasses to observe Lee's men from a distance. He noted the change in the Confederate lines, now posted on the heights behind the rust-colored creek called Antietam. The Confederate left and center were now toward the front of the Boonsboro Pike and Hagerstown Pike. Lee's extreme left rested in what was called the West Woods, to the southwest of David R. Miller's farm, and his right was anchored on a hill to the right of Sharpsburg, near Shade Farm. To McClellan's front, on the hills in the distance, he could see Confederate artillery posted there, and white clouds of smoke soon made an appearance followed by the explosions that sent dirt flying. McClellan sent his staff farther back, since it was the large group of people that most likely drew Confederate fire. He put his glasses back in their case and rode back to his main lines, directing his arriving corps to take a position.

Hooker's First Corps prepared to march shortly after the Confederate artillery barrage started that morning; however, orders to finally move out were not issued until afternoon. By the time the First Corps moved, crossing Antietam Creek by way of a ford and bridge close to Keedysville, it was after 4:00 p.m. Once across; they moved toward the direction of the Confederate left flank. McClellan hoped that moving this way and attacking the Confederate left would create a diversion in favor of the main attack on Lee's right followed by an attack in the center.[87]

Meade's and Ricketts's divisions were ordered to cross the nearest bridge while Doubleday crossed at the nearest ford. Meade's division was to deploy skirmishers, if needed, to clear a path for other advancing units. Hooker, as was the norm for him, rode close by the skirmishers. He was joined shortly after reaching the skirmishers by McClellan and his staff. Checking on Hooker's progress, Hooker informed the commanding general that

"Invasion of Maryland. General Meade's army crossing the Antietam in pursuit of Lee, July 12 / from a sketch by our special artist, E. Forbes." *Library of Congress.*

his corps was the smallest after losing nearly one thousand men at South Mountain. He estimated that he had roughly twelve thousand to thirteen thousand troops remaining "to attack the whole rebel army." Shots rang out, and Meade's skirmishers quickly answered back. Hooker determined that his First Corps had run into the advanced posts of Lee's army but pressed forward. The First Corps skirmishers continued exchanging musket fire with the Confederate pickets until dark before most of the hostilities ceased for the day. Still not in the proper position, Hooker ordered Doubleday to advance his men until they became the extreme right of their army, with the Iron Brigade settling in on J. Poffenberger's farm.[88]

Hooker's men scarcely settled in before more Confederate shots were fired at them. It was more of an annoyance than anything but kept several of the men awake all night. A few of Hooker's men returned fire, but many settled in for the needed rest. A heavy rain fell through the night, making an already bad situation worse. Seeking shelter in a nearby barn, Hooker took cover for the night. Some soldiers took shelter among the trees in the patch of woods known as the North Woods. Not far to their front, Lee's army under Jackson anchored the Confederate left. In between both armies stood Miller's Cornfield, a place where the blood would flow heavily the next morning.

5

THE BLOODIEST DAY

The night of September 16 and the early-morning hours of the next day were anything but restful. Sharp cracks of musket fire filled the atmosphere, making for an intense night with little rest—a typical night on the eve of battle. Confederate pickets, within feet from the Union line, added more stress to the lives of General Hooker's men. Many, like the Confederate soldiers under Jackson, would make the ultimate sacrifice within a few hours. There was little talk among the men as the rain came down. A courier from the commanding general came through the lines with the next day's orders.

Rest did not come any easier for the Confederates. Around 10:00 p.m. on the night of the sixteenth, General Lawton's and General Trimble's brigades moved in on the Confederate left to relieve General John B. Hood's command. Hood, feeling the pain of his worn-out troops, asked General Jackson's permission for his men to leave the front lines to build fires and make food. His division was near collapse, having had little more than coffee and green corn the past three days. Jackson agreed but ordered Hood to be ready to move at a moment's notice. His troops were given their orders. With rifles in hand, his two brigades, consisting of twenty-four hundred men, quietly marched to the rear of the lines, near a whitewashed building known as Dunker Church. Union artillery rounds were fired in their direction, and the Confederates fired back. Then came silence. Jackson ordered his cannons silenced after firing a few rounds. Sporadic musket firing would continue throughout the night with little more than annoyance for effect.[89]

Dunker Church, located near the West Woods on the Antietam battlefield. *Library of Congress.*

General Mansfield received orders to get his Twelfth Corps moving. Their orders were to go to the front line and assist Hooker's corps when needed. Mansfield's corps followed Hooker's path and set up camp in a field northeast from where Hooker's men were. Mansfield, like other corps commanders, wanted his men to get as much rest as they could before the oncoming battle.

By 3:00 a.m., the rain had turned to a downpour, continuing for another two hours. A thick fog filled the air, putting the pickets on both sides on high alert. The stars were still in the sky when Hooker's skirmishers became engaged with Jackson's men as their silhouettes began to appear. Hooker left quarters in J. Poffenberger's barn and worked his way to the southern edge of the North Woods. He made his observation and decided to continue his advance in a southward direction toward Dunker Church.

Hooker did not know the exact location of all the Confederate regiments in his front. The Confederate left was thrown back at almost a right angle; its left stretched across the Hagerstown Road. Jackson's old division was just west of the road, along with two brigades of Ewell's division led by

Brigadier General A.R. Lawton to the east of it. Trimble's brigade, led by Colonel James Walker, was on the right of the division, its right resting along the Mumma's family cemetery, and its left extending across the Smoketown Road. Trimble's brigade, from right to left, consisted of the 15th Alabama, 21st North Carolina and 21st Georgia with the 12th Georgia, resting to the left of the road. It was a total of about 700 men. On Trimble's left, Colonel Marcellus Douglas led Lawton's brigade and consisted of the 13th, 26th, 31st, 38th, 60th and 61st Georgia Regiments. In all, they numbered 1,150 men, all ready to fight and waiting for the enemy to make their move. Lawton's left rested over one hundred yards east of the Hagerstown Pike; its right faced northeast, about seventy yards from Trimble's left.[90]

Camp life. Army of the Potomac taking it easy. *Library of Congress.*

Many historians believe that the Battle of Antietam began before 6:00 a.m., give or take. It was about sixty-five degrees and humid at battle time. The humidity caused the smoke from artillery and musket fire to hang low to the ground, making it extremely difficult to see. Hooker stood at the edge of the North Woods; to his left was the East Woods, and to his right, the West Woods. General Abner Doubleday's division was the right of Hooker's line, with the brigades of Gibbon in front and Phelps directly behind. Patrick's brigade would follow Phelps but would be held back, not taking part at the start of the fight.

To the left of Doubleday, at the edge of the East Woods, Seymour's brigade of Meade's division was placed. To their rear, in support, was Duryee's brigade of Rickett's division, and behind Duryee was Christian and Hartsuff, also of Ricketts's division. The soldiers readied themselves for combat by saying last-minute prayers and having thoughts of their families. They also emptied their pockets of unwanted items, such as pipes and playing cards and anything else they did not want to have on them in case they got killed. Many soldiers did not want their families knowing they smoked, drank whiskey or played cards, as drinking and playing cards were considered sins. They shed those items as fast as possible; off in the distance was the sharp crack of small-arms fire.

The men of the Iron Brigade went into formation like the professional soldiers they were when called. Some moved more slowly than others; the slow ones had stomach pains from overeating sour apples from Joseph Poffenberger's farms. The order to advance was given, with the Wisconsin men saying their final prayers as they marched in a clearing, past the buildings that made up the Poffenberger property. Once the Iron Brigade cleared Poffenberger's barn and were just to the north of the North Woods, Confederate artillery broke the quiet march. Several shells found their marks, ripping holes among the Wisconsin ranks. Poague's Virginia Battery was placed onto a hillcrest just to the south of David R. Miller's barn. Off to the west, the Iron Brigade's movement caught the attention of Pelham's four guns on Nicodemus Hill. The scream of the incoming shells was enough to make anyone throw down their arms and run, but First Sergeant William H. Harries of Company B, 2nd Wisconsin, wanted to do all in his power to preserve the country "undivided" with the flag "unsullied." Harries, promoted to first sergeant after the fight at South Mountain, still wore corporal strips during Antietam, as his paperwork had not gone through yet. The hefty loss at South Mountain caused many privates and corporals to move up in rank at a faster pace than normal. Harries recalled that, at

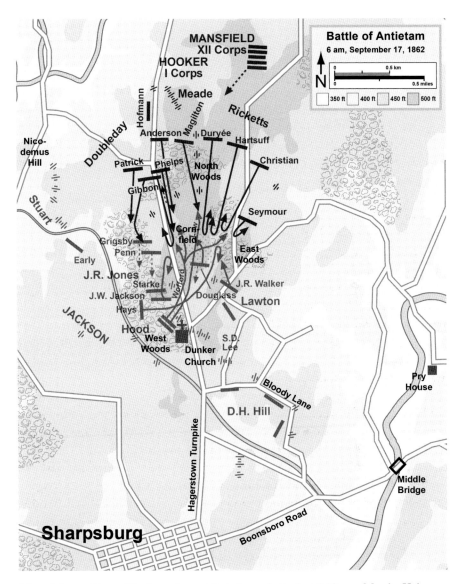

Map of the positions of both armies and their lines of attack at 6:00 a.m. Map by Hal Jespersen. *www.cwmaps.com.*

the start of the Iron Brigade's advance, "we were hungry, ragged and dirty. Before starting, we pulled up our belts a notch or two."[91]

Once in the woods, Gibbon's men passed through Meade's Pennsylvania Reserves, who had bivouacked there the night before. Colonel Walter Phelps's brigade consisting of the 22nd, 24th, 30th and 84th New York, along

"General view of the Joseph Poffenberger Farm, looking north, with (from left to right) the House, the Wash House, the Barn, the Corn Crib–Granary, the Blacksmith Shop and the Wagon Shed—Joseph Poffenberger Farm, House, 17834 Mansfield Avenue, Sharpsburg, Washington County, MD." *Library of Congress.*

with the 2nd U.S. Sharpshooters, waited until called but fell in behind the Iron Brigade. Patrick's New Yorkers were held in reserve during this time.[92]

In order to get a feel for where the Confederate line was, Gibbon ordered Lieutenant Colonel Edward S. Bragg to send out skirmishers. Company I advanced to the left into a plowed field to the front (southern side) of the North Woods, while Company C moved off to the right. The rest of the 6th Wisconsin followed close behind. Under orders Gibbon received from Hooker, the regiment, followed by the rest of the brigade, moved to the right until it reached the Hagerstown pike, then marched south. Nearing David R. Miller's garden, the Iron Brigade encountered heavy fire from Confederate skirmishers, probably from the 31st Georgia from Lawton's brigade that were in the area. The 6th Wisconsin Skirmishers, under Captain John A. Kellogg, after several exchanges of small arms fire, forced the Georgians back to the edge of the corn. The regiment then completed its advance through the North Woods before reaching the open field, where they once again came under heavy artillery fire from Pelham's guns to their right and Poague's from the front.

Harries saw Poague's Battery moving into place, but at first, he believed it was their own until it fired at them. Many Confederates were dressed in blue during this time, having taken the uniforms from the recent raid at Harpers Ferry. The first couple of shots exploded above the heads of the Iron Brigade, but the third landed in the rear of the 6th Wisconsin, killing two men and wounding eleven, "one of whom had both arms taken off." Screams and moans from the wounded filled the air, along with more bursts of artillery shells. Still, the columns advanced, with the lucky ones trying not to step on the dead and wounded. Harries, along with others from the 2nd Wisconsin, stepped to the side of a wounded captain who was crawling toward the rear, dragging a bloody stump where a foot had once been. Yelling out as loud as he could, Lieutenant Colonel Bragg, commander of the 6th Wisconsin, ordered his lines to be re-formed. At the northern edge of the North Woods, the commands shifted into regimental fronts. The 2nd Wisconsin moved to the left of the 6th, and the 7th Wisconsin moved to the left rear of the 2nd while the 19th Indiana followed behind the 6th.[93]

The 6th Wisconsin's right wing passed by Miller's garden without an issue, but the left wing was held up because of a picket fence surrounding the garden. After knocking the fence down, the left wing of the 6th was able to reunite with the right. Major Rufus Dawes called the regiment to a halt to re-form their lines. Dawes shouted out orders for the 2nd Wisconsin to re-form as well; as this order was given, he turned and looked back. Not far away was Captain Edwin A. Brown of Company E, 2nd Wisconsin. Brown was in the process of repeating Dawes's order when he went quiet—a bullet struck him in his mouth, killing him instantly.[94]

The three right companies of the 6th Wisconsin soon found themselves crowded together on the road and across it on the right. Major Dawes ordered the other regiments of the brigade that followed the 6th Wisconsin as they closed in on an open space between the orchard and cornfield. Still under heavy artillery and musket fire, Dawes ordered the troops to lie down while the Wisconsin skirmishers searched the cornfield.[95]

General Gibbon, observing that his brigade was in trouble, caught sight of a Confederate regiment moving from the West Woods toward the pike. He sent "the guns of Battery B to the front." Once in place, the six guns pounded the Confederate line with heavy shot that cut through the treetops of the West Woods, causing branches to fall on Hood's Texans, who sat happily cooking their rations of bacon and biscuits. Gibbon recalled his brigade being in what he called a "hornets' nest" without being aware of what was happening anywhere else on the battlefield.[96]

To avoid being flanked on the right, Gibbon sent orders for the 7th Wisconsin and 19th Indiana to break apart from the rest of the brigade and move to the right. Their orders were to move across the Hagerstown Pike, down a ravine and into the northern edge of the West Woods. The objective was to hopefully move in behind the Confederate regiment, probably part of Colonel A.J. Grigsby's brigade, and attack from behind. Marching toward the woods, the 7th Wisconsin and 19th Indiana encountered a few skirmishers, but after a quick exchange of musket fire, the Confederate skirmishers retreated.

To their left, men from the 7th Wisconsin and 19th Indiana saw their wounded comrades from the Iron Brigade making their way back beyond their own lines as bullets, shot and shell screamed over their heads. Around this time, other elements of Doubleday's division began their advance in overwhelming numbers. They moved south toward Jackson's weak defensive line just south of the cornfield.

Doubleday sent Phelps's brigade forward through the North Woods. Just south of the woods, in a clearing, Phelps encountered Hooker along with his staff. Hooker shouted to Phelps to speed up and support Gibbon, who was advancing near the cornfield at this time. The direct and cross artillery fire from the Confederate batteries "playing upon this field was very heavy," wrote Phelps. His brigade continued advancing, despite the artillery barrage with minimal losses. Stopping about ninety paces in advance of Company B's artillery, Phelps deployed a column to ready for battle, its right resting on the Hagerstown Pike and the line moved forward some fifty yards to the rear of Gibbon's brigade. Phelps had five regiments, the 22nd, 24th, 30th and 84th New York, along with the 2nd United States Sharpshooters. In total, Phelps had 425 men.[97]

Not long after Phelps deployed his column, the 6th Wisconsin's skirmishers, at this time in the cornfield, encountered a Confederate line to the right along the fence bordering the Hagerstown Pike. A heated musketry exchange with the Confederates quickly drove the Confederates across the pike. The rest of the 6th Wisconsin quickly followed up, along with the 2nd Wisconsin. The right wing of the 6th Wisconsin currently was on the pike, under direct command of Bragg. The 6th's left was under the command of Dawes and, along with the 2nd Wisconsin, was just entering Miller's Cornfield.

The 6th's skirmishers, for some reason, failed to clear their advance. When the 6th's right wing reached a rise of ground near Miller's barn, there were stacks of hay to the right of the road, and they came under severe musket fire from Confederate captain A.C. Page's 21st Virginia skirmishers, who were lying in wait along the edge of the West Woods. Taken by surprise, Private Franklin Gerlaugh along with his best friend Private William P. Black had little time to react. Both Gerlaugh and Black had been friends since they were small kids growing up on farms in Fredonia, Wisconsin. A month after the Civil War began, Gerlaugh could not resist and joined the army. Black, not wanting to let his friend experience all the "fun," signed up on May 10, 1861. When Page's skirmishers fired on the 6th Wisconsin, one bullet struck Gerlaugh through the forehead, going clean through. As he fell forward, his dearest friend, William P. Black, reached for him; as Black did this, a bullet struck him in the throat, killing him instantly.[98]

Near the Dunker Church, Colonel Stephen D. Lee of Lee's Artillery Battalion had his artillery in place before 3:00 a.m. on the morning of the battle. Captain William W. Parker, along with Captain P. Woolfolk, placed their batteries in front of the church, just to the right of the Hagerstown Pike. Along with Poague, Stuart's horse artillery, Parker's and Woolfolk's artillery to the north of the Dunker Church lobbed shots at the advancing Iron Brigade. Keeping up a heavy artillery fire over the heads of their infantry, Lee's artillery kept the advancing men of Doubleday's division on their toes. By this time, the air was thick with smoke; men from Lee's artillery could hardly see what they were firing at.

The skirmishers from Lawton's brigade came out of the southern end of Miller's Cornfield. He sent an order for Brigadier General Harry T. Hays to move his Louisiana Tigers to the rear of his line and prepare for an attack. General Stonewall Jackson issued an order for General Early to move his brigade off to the left flank in support of Pelham's artillery on Nicodemus Hill. Jackson, at this time, continued observing the mass amounts of Union soldiers advancing toward his lines. Shell and canister exploded all around the Federal troops, but they kept coming in droves. Jackson's men, however, held their positions "in the face of superior numbers."[99]

General Ricketts received orders to advance his Second Division and gave orders to Generals Duryee and Hartsuff to advance their brigades. Both were instructed to move to the right when they exited the East Woods and advance south. Hartsuff's Brigade led the advance with Duryee in close support. Once out of the woods, Duryee moved to the right of Hartsuff, forming a line of battle. Christian, with his Second Brigade, went directly forward, staying to the left of the Smoketown Road. Their advance was soon put to a halt when they came under heavy artillery bursts from Lee's guns near the Dunker Church. Duryee's brigade advanced down a slight incline and deployed along a fence on the north side of Miller's Cornfield.

The 107th Pennsylvania was on the right with the 97th, 104th and 105th New York on the left.

To help ease the movements of Duryee and Hartsuff's brigades, Captain James Thompson moved his light Pennsylvania Artillery, Battery C, to assist the 1st Pennsylvania Light Artillery, Battery F, under Captain Ezra W. Matthews. Already engaged against S.D. Lee's guns, Matthews became under direct assault from Trimble's infantry fire. To aid Matthews, Thompson turned his batteries on Trimble's line. Both Thompson and Matthews fired charges of cannister into Miller's Cornfield. "Taking advantage of the ground, both batteries opened with destructive effect, officers and men displaying great coolness while exposed to a severe fire of artillery and infantry," wrote Ricketts. The artillery did its job and provided the opportunity needed; Duryee's men leapt into action, bounding over the fence and through the thick corn—moving to the south edge of the field about 245 yards. The right of the line was roughly 150 yards east of the Hagerstown Pike; the left was about 100 yards from the East Woods.[100]

Duryee's men came charging through the cornstalks like a herd of cattle. Along the way, they pushed any remaining Confederate skirmishers out of the high-standing corn. Lying in wait, Colonel M. Douglass of Lawton's brigade remained vigilant for the first sign of the Union men to show. All of a sudden, Duryee's men made their appearance and Confederate muskets erupted. Ducking and taking whatever cover they could, Duryee's men fired back. After a few minutes of a heated exchange, Duryee had to pull his men back a short distance to a split-railed fence that offered a little protection just north of their current position. Ignoring all the men dropping out of the ranks, the New Yorkers kept up a hot fire on Lawton's Georgians. The body count continued to rise as both sides showed no signs of giving up. The wounded men who wore both blue and gray stood their grounds and fought with honor, each side not willing to give the other an inch of ground.

A heavy cloud of smoke hung over the southern edge of Miller's Cornfield; the body count continued to grow in the open clover field that Lawton's right and the 12th Georgia, of Trimble's brigade, fought so hard to maintain. Seeing the struggle Lawton's right and the 12th Georgia was having, Colonel James Walker of Trimble's brigade "ordered the Twenty-first Georgia and Twenty-first North Carolina Regiments to wheel to the left, and, taking shelter under a low stone fence running at right angles to their former line, direct their fire upon the wavering Yankee regiment, with the view of breaking the enemy's line at this point," wrote Walker. Walker, leading Trimble's brigade, had already been battling with Brigadier General

Truman Seymour of Meade's division for the last fifteen minutes or so but was able to maintain his ground.[101]

Unable to recover from the initial round of fire, Duryee ordered his men back through the cornfield. Skirmishers from Lawton's brigade gave chase. Brigadier General George Hartsuff's brigade surged forward in relief. Not long into the fight, Hartsuff was shot down and carried from the field, seriously wounded, but he survived. Hartsuff's brigade of Massachusetts, New York and Pennsylvania soldiers poured into Lawton's men with several volleys of musket fire. Walker's men just to the right of Lawton's brigade had little choice but to fall back. Luckily for Colonel Douglas, who saw the trouble his brigade was in, he received help from Brigadier General Harry Hays's Fighting Louisiana Tigers, who were still waiting in reserve. Douglas was killed minutes later. Hays's brigade was rather small, consisting of not more than 550 men. Once in line, the Tigers fired quickly. Several of the Tigers' rounds found their mark, but Hays's men would not last long. Hartsuff's and Seymour's Brigade, in conjunction with Thompson's and Matthew's Batteries, quickly reduced Hays's command by half.[102]

At one point, the Iron Brigade had been the First Corps advanced unit; however, once they stalled in the cornfield, Duryee's brigade took the advanced. The Iron Brigade moved along with only a few snags until Jackson's left brigade, under Grigsby, fired into the right flank of the 6th Wisconsin. At the same time, Lawton's brigade, along with the 12th Georgia, rose up and fired into Duryee's men coming out of the cornfield. Grigsby's Virginians continued a deadly fusillade of musket fire on the 6th Wisconsin, making their advance impossible. Lieutenant Colonel Bragg reported: "I discovered the enemy in force, lying in line of battle along the fence and across the field to the wood, at right angles with the road, his line being then within musket range. At the same time, he increased his fire from the woods on the right flank."[103]

The right wing of the 6th Wisconsin was now pinned between the two fences on each side of the Hagerstown Pike. Left without any options, Bragg yelled for the company in the road to lie down. Soon after his order was given, a bullet struck him in the left arm, causing a massive amount of blood loss. Bragg, losing blood fast, felt like he was about to faint. With what strength he had left, he yelled for Sergeant Major Howard J. Huntington to fetch Major Dawes. Huntington took off, dodging Confederate bullets as he scrambled into the cornfield. A short distance into the field, Huntington, out of breath, found Dawes. "Major," he yelled, "Colonel Bragg wants to see you quick at the turnpike." Immediately, Dawes sprang to his feet and raced toward the pike. He reached Bragg in time to hear him say, "Major, I am shot." Bragg fell to the ground, the loss of blood becoming too much for him to remain conscious[104]

Observing a tear in the side of Bragg's overcoat, Dawes thought he may have been shot through the body. Luckily for Bragg, he was not, and Dawes ordered two men to carry him to the rear. The major assumed command of the 6th Wisconsin, which was still under intense fire. Standing near the fence along the cornfield, he looked over the right wing of the 6th, which was still on the turnpike and firing on the Confederates in the West Woods. From his position, Dawes could see a group of mounted rebel officers who he assumed were a general with his staff. Picking up a musket, using the fence rail as a rest, Dawes fired toward the mounted Confederates. He fired five more rounds rather quickly, as a group of his men were handing him loaded muskets. Scattering, the mounted Confederates disappeared into the woods.[105]

Artillery shells and bullets shrieked through the air at the Iron Brigade from the front and their right. Confederate skirmishers from Lawton's and Trimble's brigades slipped back into the cornfield between the two leading Union brigades and shot them at close range. Members of the 2nd Wisconsin fired back into the stalks of corn; a few bullets found their marks, staining the dark green stalks with blood. Private Elon Brown returned fire; as he pulled the rod off his musket out to reload, a Confederate bullet struck him in the shoulder, knocking him to the ground. "If I had been half an inch taller, it would have hurt me pretty bad," Brown wrote to his brothers and sisters. Also wounded in the same volley was Sergeant William H. Harries, who was struck in the left part of his chest. First Sergeant Walker S. Rouse, also of Company E, assisted Harries getting up and pointed him toward the rear. Rouse survived the Battle of Antietam but died of wounds received at Gettysburg less than a year later.[106]

Gibbon discovered that a good number of Jackson's artillery were not in the West Woods but were located on open ground to the northwest of Alfred Poffenberger's barn. Poague's, Brockenbrough and D'Aquin's batteries followed where the infantry went earlier that morning and were still there. Poague's was near Grigsby's line, while Brockenbrough was placed in front of Starke's brigade with Captain D'Aquin near Brockenbrough. All batteries continued hurling shells at the cornfield, causing severe damage among the ranks and to Duryee's and Hartsuff's brigades as well.

Poague, after firing several rounds of shells, became a hot target for the skirmishers of the 6th Wisconsin and had little choice but to relocate to a position behind Grigsby's line. From his new position, Poague's battery lobbed canister into the cornfield. Gibbon ordered Stewart's two guns of Battery B to the front; Doubleday around the same time ordered the advance of Patrick's brigade to assist the 7th Wisconsin and the 19th Indiana. Union batteries across the Antietam to the east, now with the assistance of Stewart's artillery, finally provided a window for the 6th and 2nd Wisconsin to move.

The left wing of the 6th Wisconsin advanced and busted through the remainder of the cornfield and into an open field beyond. Dawes ordered the right wing of the 6th to guide left and move through the cornfield. Noticing three companies of the 6th Wisconsin were not following, Dawes sent Sergeant Major Huntington to find Captain Kellogg and find the problem. Off Huntington went, through the heavily damaged cornfield; stalks that once stood tall were now broken in half or hung from one side or another. Between the canister and musket balls, Miller's Cornfield, as far as a useable crop, was a loss. Huntington soon found Kellogg on the ground using whatever he could for cover. He was unable to move the three Wisconsin companies currently; the Confederate fire coming from the West woods was too heavy.

Not happy with the answer he received, Dawes once again ordered Huntington to carry the message to Kellogg. This time, he ordered him to move and use the cornfield as cover. Huntington delivered the message, stood up and made a break for the cornfield. As he did this, a Confederate bullet struck him, knocking him senseless. Badly bruised, Huntington regained his footing and continued back to Dawes. Kellogg gave the order to move; the men from Grigsby's brigade threw another deadly volley at the Wisconsin men, killing many of them. Once again, Kellogg ordered his men prone and to wait for the right moment to move. The three companies of the 6th quickly returned fire and broke for the cover of the cornfield. With the 2nd Wisconsin on the 6th's left, they reached the south edge of Miller's Cornfield. To their surprise, about two hundred yards in front, a long line of men in butternut and gray belonging to Lawton's brigade stood and, with a deadly fire, did severe damage to the men of the 6th and 2nd Wisconsin. Corporal Charles W. Delany of Company G, 2nd Wisconsin, had a bullet go clean through his hat, singeing a straight line through his hair.[107]

From where he stood, Dawes could see the Dunker Church— the ordered objective was in clear view. "Men, I cannot say fell; they were knocked out of the ranks by dozens," Dawes recalled. He ordered the troops to press on, both the 6th and 2nd Wisconsin continued advancing toward their objective, firing and reloading as fast as they could.

Taking on heavy fire from west of the pike, both the 6th and 2nd Wisconsin slightly wheeled to the right, leaving the left wing of the 2nd Wisconsin taking fire from both Taliaferro's brigade—made up of both Virginia and Alabama infantry from Jones's division to the west in an "unprecedented iron storm"—and Lawton's brigade to the south. Shear panic had set in by this point. Men from both sides were tearing into cartridges with their teeth as fast as they could. Some men even took the responsibility of doing all the reloading while the man in front fired. Sweat, along with the smoke from the guns, added to the burning sensation of the men's eyes, hurting their shooting accuracy. Confederate general J.R. Jones, who had been watching the exchange of gunfire from his position west of the Hagerstown Pike, was removed from the field after a union artillery shell exploded a few feet above his head. He was knocked to the ground senseless before regaining his wits and turning command over to General Starke.[108]

Meanwhile, Patrick's brigade followed the 7th Wisconsin across the pike and went into formation behind the 19th Indiana. Both the 19th Indiana and 7th Wisconsin pushed their way into the West Woods with bullets whizzing over the heads of many of the troops and artillery rounds sending dirt flying as the shells landed and exploded. Captain Page, who just a short time earlier had surprised the right wing of the 6th Wisconsin with his 21st Virginia, was now forced to fall back. However, Page's men were reinforced by Captain J.E. Penn, also of Jones's brigade. Before Jones had been wounded, he ordered Penn to guard the left flank; but, shortly after becoming engaged, Penn himself was wounded, losing a leg. His Virginians soon fell back to the main Confederate lines deeper in the woods behind Starke's left.

Both the 7th Wisconsin and 19th Indiana came to a standstill upon reaching a rail fence a short way into the woods. Men from Penn's regiment poured one last deadly volley into both regiments of the Iron Brigade as they stalled. Ordering his men to tear the fence down, Captain John B. Callis then commanded his men to quickly return fire. Some of the 7th Wisconsin were too eager to fight and just climbed over the fence and charged after the retreating Confederates. However, they came to a halt when Penn's men rallied and forced the 7th back, "making havoc in our ranks." Luckily for the 7th Wisconsin and 19th Indiana, Patrick's brigade came up and rendered aid. The 7th Wisconsin backtracked to the place where they had entered the West Woods and watched their right flank. Callis kept his regiment there until Confederate artillery began firing rounds of "canister into our ranks with terrible effect." With little choice, the 7th pulled back farther into a "cover of an elevation of land covered with timber" and waited for the remainder of the brigade, Callis remembered.[109]

From the location of the 2nd and 6th Wisconsin, Confederates could be seen swarming out of the West Woods, just to the north of the Dunker Church. There was no doubt the intent was to force back the Union's right flank. It was Hood's Texans, and they were mad as hornets. With the 6th and 2nd Wisconsin now facing southwest toward the pike on higher ground, the 6th Wisconsin was stretched out in a long line. Kellogg's men had all been brought up finally and assisted in pushing Lawton's Georgians back until reaching cover. The Georgians managed to hold out until Hood was able to become engaged. Several men of the 6th Wisconsin tried to break and take cover in the cornfield, only to be cut down in a hail of bullets. To the north and across the pike by the haystacks where Page's men had surprised the 6th Wisconsin earlier, General Gibbon set up Battery B and, within moments, was able to aid in taking some pressure off the 6th and 2nd Wisconsin. Gibbon himself took part in firing the cannons, his face black from the powder.[110]

Starke's brigade consisted of about 650 men, while Taliaferro's was around 500. By the time Grigsby sent word to Starke that he needed help, his lines had shrunk considerably. When Starke arrived with his brigade, he found Grigsby's men lying down in the woods, taking cover from the return fire of the 6th and 2nd Wisconsin. Grigsby's men had fallen back. Stark ordered his men forward and advanced along with Taliaferro's, whose right was already resting on the Hagerstown Pike facing the Iron Brigade. Starke's focus was the southwestern corner of Miller's Cornfield, the same location where the 6th and 2nd Wisconsin forced Lawton's Georgians through. Seeing the two Confederate brigades advancing on the Wisconsin regiments, Gibbon directed artillery fire at them. One shell hit the rail fence on the west side of the pike, sending splintering wood pieces everywhere and stunning Major Dawes at the closeness of the shot.[111]

Within seconds of Gibbon's last shot, Starke was mortally wounded and died later in the day. The Confederate ranks became thinner with each step they took toward the Wisconsin brigades. By the time Starke's and Taliaferro's brigades were within forty-five yards of Wisconsin's position, Phelps's men came dashing out of the cornfield to assist the Wisconsin men. The 14th Brooklyn led the way and merged with Wisconsin with a deadly volley. Dozens more of the charging Confederates fell. "The musketry fire at this point was very heavy, but the two brigades appeared to hold their position easily," wrote Phelps. Even with thinning ranks, the remaining men of Starke's and Taliaferro's brigades continued advancing and climbing over the remaining rail fence at the Hagerstown Pike. Around this time, more aid arrived for the Wisconsin men; the 2nd U.S. Sharpshooters took their position on the right of the 6th Wisconsin at the rail fence. They opened an accurate, deadly fire on Starke's left flank, consisting of the 1st Louisiana.[112]

About an hour had passed since the bloody Battle of Antietam had begun; already, the ground around the cornfield and West Woods was covered with dead and wounded from both sides. The green stalks of corn that still stood were now stained with the blood from the brave soldiers who gave the ultimate sacrifice. Off to the south, the whitewashed church that rested near the once quiet West Woods was now riddled with bullet holes. Wounded men crawled over their fallen comrades, yelling out for help; many would not reach help in time and died on the battlefield. Confederate private Spencer G. Welch told his family in a letter that "it is useless for me to tell you of the shocking scenes I have witnessed."[113]

A line of men in blue surged forward and pushed the men of Starke's brigade back across the pike. Phelps's brigade moved forward again, this time taking a position on the left of the 2nd U.S. Sharpshooters. The Wisconsin regiments meanwhile fell back into the cornfield, regrouped and reformed their lines. At this time, the Confederates, who had already climbed the rail fence and made it onto the pike, fired off an effective volley, striking Private Wellington Bridge of Company E, 2nd Wisconsin, in the chest, killing him. Privates Vincent Flanigan and Timothy Connor, both of 2nd Wisconsin, were also killed. Those who were not injured answered back with a fire so severe that Starke's men advanced no farther; however, they maintained their position at the fence.[114]

Loud explosions sent dirt flying; bullets thudded into the dead and wounded who lay on the battlefield. The 6th and 2nd Wisconsin held their lines and showed considerable strength and will to fight to the death. However, ammunition started running low, and the men became exhausted. The humidity of the day started taking its toll. Screams and cries from the men were barely heard over the noise of artillery and musket shots. Many of the Wisconsin men were injured during the bloody engagement but refused to give up. One such man was Private Ossman Taplin from Company E, 2nd Wisconsin. Taplin had been shot earlier in the fight but remained in the ranks until becoming wounded again. He was relieved of duty and taken to a nearby field hospital, where he died a few days later. In a letter to Private Taplin's father, Corporal J.B. David wrote: "His pulse was weakened, and he could not lay easy in any position. His mouth would not open; his jaws were locked. He died about twelve minutes past three on September 24, 1862."[115]

Shortly after the Georgians were driven back, Lieutenant Colonel Thomas Allen of the 2nd Wisconsin ordered a change in his front to a right oblique position and ordered his men to build up a barricade quickly. The 6th Wisconsin was still to the 2nd's right, with its right three companies back on the pike. With ammunition running dangerously low, Major Dawes did not have much hope of holding the current position. The artillery relief from Battery B began to slow as artillery rounds grew low. Captain Joseph Campbell of Battery B was struck down with a musket ball to the shoulder, but before leaving the ranks, he was able to get off another deadly shot of cannister into Starke's ranks.

Gibbon's deadly Battery B inflicted heavy damage on Starke's Louisiana's left flank. Bodies littered the ground, with some stacking up along the pike's fence rail. These were the bodies of some of the best men the South had to offer, who gave their all and were proudly serving the 10th Louisiana Infantry. Falling like a line of dominos with every shot fired by Battery B, there was no way Starke's brigade could hold much longer.

Meanwhile, the 7th Wisconsin, 19th Indiana and Patrick's brigade managed to push farther into the northern half of the West Woods. "We have every reason to believe that our fire was very effective in repulsing their attack," wrote Captain William W. Dudley of the 19th Indiana. He had no idea just how true this was. Both his regiment and the 7th Wisconsin were able to cause Penn's regiment to retreat in haste, causing mass confusion. Now, positioned in a slight gully at the bottom of a wooded hill, the regiments were unable to see what was over the hill.[116]

On other parts of the field, Lieutenant Colonel J. William Hoffman's brigade, under Doubleday, remained on Joseph Poffenberger's farm with several of the division's batteries. It was these batteries that had silenced Pelham's artillery on Nicodemus Hill. Reynolds and Matthews, along with four of Campbell's guns, remained in position between the Poffenberger's and D.R. Miller's farm and the East Woods. Meanwhile, the batteries of Ransom moved along with Magilton and Anderson's brigades, from Meade's division, from the North Woods to the front, while Christian's brigade, consisting of the 26th and 94th New York and the 88th and 90th Pennsylvania, moved in support of Seymour and Hartsuff. Both were still involved in a fight at the southeast corner of Miller's Cornfield and the East Woods.

Colonel Peter Lyle of Christian's brigade recorded the following events:

> *We moved to the right, passed to the front through a cornfield, and took a position on the left of Matthews' battery, First Pennsylvania, which we were ordered to support. Here we were exposed to a severe fire of musketry and shell, we being immediately in rear of the skirmishers, who were engaging the enemy in the cornfield in front. We were moved to the left behind a wood and formed in close column. The shells falling around us, the battery was moved to the front, into the woods. Here we were subject to a raking fire of grape, canister, and shell. The battery fell back, and the regiment was deployed and moved to the front in line.*[117]

The 26th and 94th New York moved south through the woods before crossing the Smoketown Road and set up a defensive line behind a fence on the south edge of the woods. Just as the two regiments reached the fence, several shots of cannister ripped through their ranks from the direction of the Mumma Farm. Musket fire from General Ripley's brigade, from D.H. Hill's division, also caused destruction among the New York ranks. Ripley's brigade took a position to the right of Trimble's men between the Mumma graveyard and Smoketown Road. Hartsuff's left end of his line also came under fire; the 83rd New York received assistance from the 88th Pennsylvania. Both sides clashed, leaving the bodies of the men where they fell. Christian's regiments were able to observe the fronts of Lawton and Hays and see the Iron Brigade, along with Phelps's brigade, fighting it out against Starke's men. Unable to communicate with their superiors during the complete confusion that reigned on the field, lower-grade officers had to maneuver and respond to the situation on their own initiatives.[118]

Near the Dunker Church, Hood's Texans sat around their campfires cooking their first hot meal in three days. The annoying Union artillery shells exploding over their heads was a minor inconvenience to put up with in order to have something other than green corn and apples. Sadly for the Texans, many would not get the chance to eat one last cooked meal. General Lawton had been hit, and Hood was "to come forward as soon as possible." The anger the Texans felt would soon be known; after forming into ranks, they began screaming and hollering like a bunch of mad men and set off in advance to face an "immense force of the enemy." Hood's Division, consisting of General's Law and Wofford's Brigades, advanced toward the cornfield to replace the badly mangled units belonging to Starke and Taliaferro. Lawton's brigade had already begun pulling back after an intense fight with the 2nd and 6th Wisconsin.[119]

Things had been progressing nicely for Gibbon's and Phelps's men, but the soldiers of the 2nd and the 6th began to tire, and the air had not cleared of smoke. Seeing whom to shoot at became a major problem, and remaining along the western edge of the cornfield, the soldiers could move no farther. They halted their advance, pouring volley after deadly volley into Starke and Taliaferro's men. The Iron Brigade, along with the aid of Phelps, had caused a massive amount of damage in the Confederate ranks, leaving no other option but for the two Confederate brigades to start pulling back. Although it was a pleasant sight for the Wisconsin men, things were about to take a turn for the worse. Coming out of the West Woods near the Dunker Church were Hood's men, and they were mad as hornets.

The long line making up Hood's division charged out of the woods in a large wave. They fired on the move, advancing faster toward the Iron Brigade, which by this time had run low on ammunition. Both the 2nd and 6th Wisconsin and Phelps's men returned fire. Soon, the fighting became "the most terrible clash of arms, by far, that has occurred during the war," Hood recalled. Through the smoke, the Wisconsin men could hear the screech of the Rebel yell grow closer each passing second. There was no time to aim; picking a target was out of the question, since none could be seen. Law's men (the 2nd and 11th Mississippi and the 6th North Carolina) moved on the right down the Smoketown Road toward the East Woods. The Texas Brigade (the 18th Georgia, Hampton's Legion and the 1st, 4th and 5th Texas) followed close behind.[120]

As Law's brigade advanced, they received a volley from Hartsuff's brigade about halfway through the open field, just south of the cornfield. Law's men answered back without hesitation. Racing across the Hagerstown Pike with Hampton's Legion on the left flank, then the 18th Georgia and the 1st Texas reached the open field south of Miller's Cornfield and racked the ranks of the 2nd and 6th Wisconsin with a hot masking fire. Left without a choice, both Wisconsin regiments fired back before disappearing back into the cornfield. Battery B, from its position along the Hagerstown Pike, delivered case rounds into the left flank of Hood's line. Recovering, the South Carolinians making up Hampton's Legion charged toward the cornfield.

By this time, the only remaining Union troops left in the cornfield were the wounded, dead or ones who became separated from their regiments. Those Wisconsin men lucky enough to escape were ordered to halt along the Hagerstown Pike just west of the cornfield. "I gathered my men on the turnpike, reorganized them, and reported to General Doubleday," said Major Dawes. Doubleday ordered Dawes to take both the 2nd and the 6th Wisconsin back to the North Woods and wait for further orders. During this time, the 1st Texas made its way through the cornfield and began firing on the retreating Wisconsin men, inflicting little damage to the men but causing severe damage to the surrounding trees.[121]

Hartsuff's brigade had not been actively fighting for long before suffering at the hands of Trimble's, Ripley's and Hays's men. The right and center of his lines had already fallen back, as had Seymour's and parts of Christian's brigade, at the sight of Hood's hard-charging brigade. It would not be long before the only Union regiment left east of the cornfield was the 90th Pennsylvania. "We passed through the woods into a plowed field, where we engaged the enemy until our forces on the right and left gave way, when, having but about 100 men left, we fell back slowly and in good order, under cover of the woods, and then, being hard pressed by the enemy," wrote Colonel Lyle.[122]

Trimble's, Hays's and Lawton's men were also done fighting, having run dangerously low on ammunition and suffered heavy losses. They worked their way back to the main Confederate line after part of Hood's Brigade advanced closer to them. To aid the Union men's fall back, artillery from across the Antietam and north of the cornfield opened fire. Several of the rounds found their mark, wiping out scores of Hood's men. The 5th Texas and 4th Alabama shrugged off the explosions and continued chasing the retreating Federals into the East Woods. "So far, we had been entirely successful, and everything promised a decisive victory," reported Colonel E.M. Law.[123]

With the 90th Pennsylvania left by itself, it poured several rounds of musket balls into Law's charging men. The heated exchange lasted several minutes before the 90th realized that everyone on their left and right had already pulled back. Constant effective fire from Law's men was more than the 90th could handle, and they too began to pull back, firing rounds as fast as they could as they entered the East Woods. The 4th Alabama was right on their heels, firing as they pushed through the woods. Not ready to retire yet, the 21st Georgia, of Trimble's brigade, followed the 4th Alabama into the East Woods after the retiring Federals. Not far into the woods, both the Alabama and Georgia regiments bumped into the 6th Pennsylvania Reserves, which had been on its way to the front to lend assistance. Shortly after a heavy gunfight, the tired, worn-out 6th Pennsylvania, who had been involved in the fight since the battle opened, pulled back into a defensive position. Now, the 5th Texas made its way toward the fight and, along with the 4th Alabama and the Georgians, dug in.[124]

On the other side of the cornfield, along the Hagerstown Pike, the men under Phelps, the 2nd and the 6th Wisconsin, had pulled back to Campbell's battery, where the wounded men were taken farther to the rear to the safety of the North Woods. In the cornfield itself, the 1st Texas remained firing shots at Anderson's brigade, of Meade's division, who had come to halt the Texans' advance. Meanwhile, the 18th Georgia, Hampton's Legion, and the 4th Texas, who remained in the open clover field to the south of Miller's Cornfield, wheeled left and faced the Hagerstown Pike. Colonel Wofford described what happened next:

> *Riding back to the left of our line, I found the fragment of the Eighteenth Georgia Regiment in front of the extreme right battery of the enemy, located on the pike running by the church, which now opened upon our thinned ranks a most destructive fire. The men and officers were gallantly shooting down the gunners, and for a moment silenced them. At this time the enemy's fire was most terrific, their first line of infantry having been driven back to their guns, which now opened a furious fire, together with their second line of infantry, upon our thinned and almost annihilated ranks.[125]*

The infantry mentioned was the 7th Wisconsin and the 19th Indiana, along with Patrick's brigade in support. They had finally come up from the gully in the West Woods. Once in sight of Wofford's men, the remainder of the Iron Brigade and Campbell's battery showered them in a hail of bullets and artillery cannister. After replenishing their ammunition, the 2nd and 6th Wisconsin went and aided Campbell's Battery, along with the 23rd and 80th New York from Patrick's brigade. A strong defensive front of Wisconsin and New York men, along with an accurate battery, had severely damaged Hood's brigade to the point where they could not remain for long. "Our brigade having suffered so greatly, I was satisfied they could neither advance nor hold their position," wrote Wofford. He rode back to make General Hood aware of the situation; not having much choice, he ordered his men to pull back. The defensive line his regiments made against the 7th Wisconsin and 19th Indiana gave way, sending them back "under cover of the woods to the left of the church," Wofford said.[126]

To the east, Law's 2nd Mississippi, 11th Mississippi and 6th North Carolina were fighting the part of Magilton's brigade that had yet to pull back. Running low on ammunition and suffering high losses, Law ordered his left wing to fall back quickly toward the safety of the Dunker Church. Off to their right, the 4th Alabama, 21st Georgia and 5th Texas were still holding a defensive line in the East Woods. Off in the distance, they observed a massive amount of men in blue marching in their general direction from the north. It was elements of the Union's Twelfth Corps arriving just in time to replace the worn-out Union troops who had opened the battle. While concerned about what was coming at them, the men of Law's brigade remained in place, conserving ammunition and allowing the rest of the smoke to clear.

While the remainder of the Texans were reorganizing on the Smoketown Road, General Ripley's brigade fully entered the fight. Until this time, they had been lying low in a plowed field near the Mumma Farm, where they had fired distant rounds into the East Woods but had not fully engaged. From their location, they were under heavy Union artillery fire from across Antietam Creek; their position, which Ripley was ordered to occupy, was "in full view of nearly all" of the Union's batteries. The constant shelling tore major holes in the ranks of Ripley's men, inflicting "serious loss" even before being called into action. Prior to going into action, Ripley ordered a few of his men to set nearby farm buildings on fire to prevent Union troops from using them. Just before 8:00 a.m., Ripley received word to advance; he gave the order, and his "troops sprung to their arms with alacrity" and moved past the burning buildings, then re-formed his lines on the other side.[127]

Initially, Ripley advanced his men toward the direction of the East Woods, but he received orders from D.H. Hill to shift and move to the left toward the direction of Miller's Cornfield. As Ripley gave the order for his men to make the shift, he was struck in the neck by a bullet. Although it was a serious wound, Ripley would survive. Command was given to Colonel George Doles of the 4th Georgia Regiment. Doles moved his command toward the cornfield to fill the gap left by Law and Wofford. At the same time, at the Mumma Farm, Colonel Colquitt formed his men to follow in support of Doles.

Back along the Hagerstown Pike, the 19th Indiana, along with the 21st and the 35th New York, remained in place, facing east toward the cornfield. The 7th Wisconsin pulled back to where they first entered the West Woods to protect the right flank from the enemy. When Ripley's brigade, now led by Doles, neared the location of the 19th Indiana and the New York regiments, they fired into the 1st North Carolina's left. Shortly after the Indiana brigade fired their volley, the remnants of Starke's brigade, which had squared off early with the Iron Brigade, fired into the exposed right flank of the 19th Indiana. Taken completely by surprise, the 19th Indiana, along with Patrick's regiments, retreated across the pike and slowly moved north until they rejoined the 7th Wisconsin. After remaining in place for a short time, Confederate artillery fire from Pelham's guns threw grape and canister shot into their ranks "with terrible effect." Leaving no other choice but to abandon their positions, they pulled farther back to the North Woods, where they rejoined the rest of the brigade. The Iron Brigade was done.[128]

Patrick's men held out a little longer, covering the retreat of the Iron Brigade as they moved back to the safety of the North Woods. Patrick ordered his men to fall back, which they did, in the area of the Miller barn, and waited for ammunition and any help that could be sent. The rest of Ripley's brigade, the 4th and 44th Georgia and 3rd North Carolina exchanged shots with Anderson's Pennsylvania (9th, 11th and 12th) Regiments, who made a defensive line on the southern side of Miller's Cornfield. During this time, except for Patrick's brigade and a few of Magilton's men in the northern part of the East Woods, Hooker's First Corps was pretty much done with the fight.

It was hardly 8:00 a.m. when the once quiet rolling hills of a small Maryland town were turned into fields of slaughter. The massive clash of armies left death and destruction wherever they went; the small farming town of Sharpsburg would be no different. With the fighting going on by this time for just a little more than two hours, the soldiers who had been engaged in the fight were tired, hot and hungry. There was hardly a place to the front of Jackson's line that was not covered with the dead and wounded. Men begged for help, some with wounds so massive that it gave the survivors nightmares for months to come. For the men of Ripley's and Colquitt's brigades, having more than a full day's rest, they were ready for a fight. With Ripley's men engaged with parts of Anderson's Pennsylvania regiments, Colquitt's brigade began to move along the Mumma Farm lane toward the East Woods. Although rested and wanting to fight, they soon would find themselves outnumbered.

Just two days prior to the Battle of Antietam, Brigadier General Joseph Mansfield was given command of the Union's Twelfth Corps. Promoted to major general during the clash on South Mountain, Mansfield proved to be an asset to the Union army. Arriving before 3:00 a.m. on the morning of September 17, Mansfield's Corps had crossed Antietam Creek by way of the upper bridge. After all were across, orders were given for his men to halt and get as much rest as possible; battle would take place within a few short hours. Mansfield positioned his army about a mile to the rear of Hooker's First Corps and rested until orders were issued to move.

By the time the sun had begun to rise, the sound of cannons broke the stillness and woke most of the men. No one had time to make their morning coffee or put much of any food in their stomachs before setting out toward the sound of fighting. Still exhausted by the lack of sleep, Private William T. Leonard of Company G, 3rd Wisconsin Regiment, fought off the aches and pains brought on by the long marches. While engaged in battle, Leonard was shot in the left thigh. The bullet had passed through his hip and shattered much of his bone, leaving him "lame" and often after long marches.[129]

Approaching from the northeast, Mansfield directed his corps not to waste time, and with the sound of battle growing louder, he directed skirmishers to advance. Out of all the corps that made up the Army of the Potomac, the Twelfth had been the smallest, with about 7,500 men total. Brigadier General George H. Gordon's brigade led the way past the wounded soldiers from Hooker's Corps through the North Woods. Gordon's Third Brigade, of the First Division, consisted of the 27th Indiana, 2nd Massachusetts, 107th New York, 3rd Wisconsin and 13th New Jersey. Behind him was Brigadier General Samuel Crawford's First Brigade, made up of the 10th Maine, 28th New York and the 46th, 124th, 125th and 128th Pennsylvania. The rest of the corps followed close behind, with Brigadier General George S. Green's Second Division closely behind Crawford.[130]

Advancing as quickly as his men could move, Gordon was greeted by one of Hooker's aides, who begged him to move faster. "It was apparent, from the steady approach of the sound of musketry, that the enemy were advancing," wrote Gordon. They crossed the Smoketown Road, then moved west a short way before swinging to the left. With this move, Crawford's brigade was now the advanced brigade. Coming under the fire of Stephen D. Lee's guns, the brigades spread out a bit. Their advance had slowed somewhat as a result of Lee's artillery fire from his guns near the Dunker Church.

The 124th Pennsylvania, as they exited the North Woods, broke apart from the rest of Crawford's brigade and moved west along the south side of the North Woods toward the Hagerstown Pike. At the same time the 124th Pennsylvania broke away, so did the 10th Maine, who moved across the Smoketown Road, moving toward the direction of the East Woods. Not long after crossing the road, men from the 10th Maine began dropping, many killed instantly. Still in place from fighting earlier, the 4th Alabama from Law's Brigade, with the 5th Texas of Wofford's brigade and the 21st Georgia, fired a deadly volley when the Maine men drew near. Running dangerously low on ammunition, the remaining regiments from Hood's division could not hold their ground. The left of the 10th Maine took immediate cover behind a stone ledge, with the right half using whatever small trees they could find.

He died later from his wounds.

Confederate dead in front of Dunker Church on the Antietam battlefield. *Library of Congress.*

During this time, the 28th New York and 46th Pennsylvania moved to the right and entered Miller's field and moved toward the 4th Alabama's left. The 128th was also advancing, with the 125th Pennsylvania to their right; the 128th tried getting through the field quickly and into the cornfield. While making a valid attempt, it would not work out. The 4th Alabama fired into the 128th and cut them to pieces. General Mansfield, who had been riding near the 10th Maine Regiment, observed the Maine men firing back. But, knowing that the 128th Pennsylvania had veered off to the right, Mansfield became concerned that the 10th Maine was firing into them. Mansfield ordered the 10th Maine to hold their fire, telling them they are firing into their own men. He was mistaken. Barely getting those words out of his mouth, Mansfield and his horse were shot. He died later from his wounds.[131]

Over at Miller's Cornfield, the fighting continued, with Ripley's brigade doing their best to kill every man from Anderson's brigade. The First Corps had hardly any fight left by the time the Twelfth Corps were able to take over the fight in the East Woods and the cornfield. Now, without a corps commander, the Twelfth had to fight pretty much on their own. Both sides had been pretty much ripped to shreds by 8:00 a.m., and with the Twelfth Corps engaging the fight, Jackson's left was in need of help. Although Ripley's and Colquitt's brigades were rested, a short time ago, Ripley's men, led by Doles, would soon struggle. Colquitt up to this point has yet to fully engage in the fight, but that changed quickly.

No longer able to hold their position, the 11th and 12th Pennsylvania began to fall back out of the cornfield. The 3rd and part of the 1st North Carolina had put up a deadly fight when they advanced forward closer to the Cornfield with the right of the 3rd North Carolina near the East Woods. However, to the left of the 3rd North Carolina was part of the 1st, and they were stopped by the stubborn 9th Pennsylvania, who still held their ground. Ripley's men were not halted long, though, as the 9th Pennsylvania, outnumbered and running dangerously low on ammunition, also pulled back. The Confederate line slowly advanced, and, as it did, the 1st North Carolina pulled back and reformed to the left of the 4th Georgia.

Following the exit of the Pennsylvania regiments from the cornfield, the 3rd North Carolina had little time to enjoy their victory. The 128th Pennsylvania arrived and came charging at the 3rd North Carolina as they were about to change direction and move toward General Green's division. Turning in confusion, the 3rd North Carolina pulled back a short distance before rallying and forcing the 128th Pennsylvania to stop its assault. Falling back into the cornfield, the 3rd North Carolina sent skirmishers after them, but their main body was left on open ground and soon came under fire from Gordon's brigade.[132]

Brigadier General Alpheus Williams took command of the Twelfth Corps and ordered the 128th Pennsylvania to pull farther back as Colquitt's Brigade came into sight. Colquitt was moving toward the cornfield and was just passing the southern corner of the East Woods when it was spotted. Colquitt's men were just passing the East Woods when they encountered the 4th Alabama. Having run fully out of ammunition, they retreated and rejoined the rest of Law's brigade near the Dunker Church; however, the 6th North Carolina, under Major Robert F. Webb, took its former position on the left of the 21st Georgia. As for the rest of Ripley's brigade, they were barely holding on by this point. Having suffered heavy losses and dwindling ammunition, they could not hold their position much longer.

Gordon's brigade at this time had continued advancing through a plowed field south of the North Woods and were approaching the north side of

Miller's Cornfield. Dunbar's artillery helped pave the way for Gordon's men by throwing loads of cannister at Ripley's brigade. It proved to be too much for Ripley's men; part of the 1st North Carolina along with the 4th and 44th Georgia retreated south back toward D.H. Hill's artillery. Luckily for those retreating Confederates, Colquitt's brigade arrived, taking pressure off the retreat. The other part of the 1st North Carolina and the 3rd North Carolina remained in position for the time. Colquitt's brigade marched past the two North Carolina regiments into what was left of the cornfield and formed their line of battle with the 6th Georgia on the right of his line at a slight right angle. To the 6th's left were the 27th, 23rd and 28th Georgia, and the left of the line was anchored by the 13th Alabama.[133]

The 6th Georgia would soon come under fire from several different regiments. The right half of the regiment would square off with parts of

Illustration of dead in front of Dunker Church on the Antietam battlefield. *Library of Congress.*

Lieutenant Colonel Hector Tyndale's First Brigade, of Green's Second Division, while the 6th's left half of the line would tangle with parts of the 27th Indiana and the 3rd Wisconsin. Since the 6th and 27th Georgia were the first two regiments of Colquitt's Brigade to get into position, they came under immediate fire from not only the 27th Indiana and the 3rd Wisconsin, but also the 2nd Massachusetts, who formed their regiment at a left angle directly behind the 124th Pennsylvania, just East of the Hagerstown Pike.

While advancing to their line of battle, Private William Roberts, of C Company of the 3rd Wisconsin, made the following observations.

> *The men of the 2nd Massachusetts were on their right, and the 27th Indiana on their left. The soldiers reached the end of a stubble field, which sloped gently downward so that the Confederates they faced were about fifteen or twenty feet lower than they were. About a hundred yards in front of them was a rail fence, beyond which was another field, bordered on both west and east forests. The previous day it contained a full growth of corn, but now it was cut down by bullets and trampled by men and horses until no vestige of the crop remained.*[134]

It was not long before the fight between Gordon's brigade and Colquitt's men turned into a heated exchange. Both sides fired accurately into one another. Men melted away, causing gaps in the once filled ranks. For Jackson's men, this became a major concern. There were few men left to spare. But for the Union, this was not an issue. Soon, the Second Corps would arrive and, if needed, the Sixth Corps was held in reserve, waiting for orders to advance. They would not be needed, however; McClellan's army put up a stubborn fight that changed the way the Union fought for the rest of the Civil War.

The 27th Indiana's battle line was near what remained of the cornfield and refused their line on the left, so it was in the shape of an L. "The firing was very heavy on both sides and must have continued for two hours without any change of position on either side," said Colonel Silas Colgrove of the 27th Indiana. The 27th Georgia tried inching forward a little toward the 3rd Wisconsin, firing rapidly as they did so. Although the 27th Georgia gained a slight edge, they did not hold their new ground for long. Union artillery from Ransom and Reynolds ripped apart the Georgians, forcing many to lie down. By this time, the 3rd Wisconsin had sustained heavy losses, since their position was on a slight rise of ground, making them easier to see than other regiments.[135]

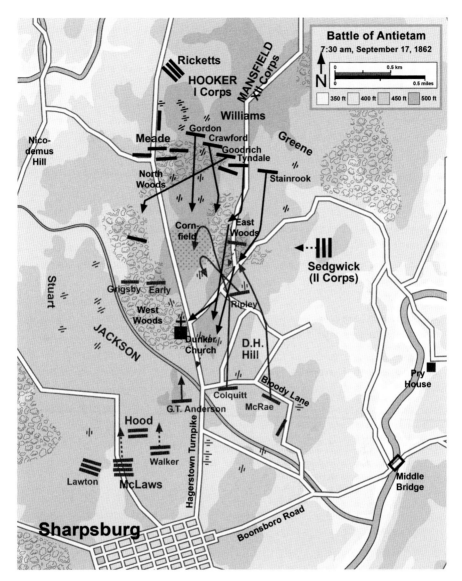

Map of both armies' positions after an hour and a half of fighting, 7:30 p.m. Map by Hal Jespersen. *www.cwmaps.com.*

After just a few minutes of fighting, Samuel Garland's North Carolina brigade crossed the Smoketown Road. The help was needed to aid Colquitt's brigade, along with the 1st and 3rd North Carolina regiments, who remained in position behind Colquitt. Over in the East Woods, the remaining Confederates from Law's brigade were also happy to see the men from North Carolina. Garland's North Carolina brigade was led into action by Colonel Duncan McRae of the Fifth North Carolina Infantry. McRae moved his men by the left flank, passing the southern part of the East Woods, McRae ordered his men to form a line of battle. The joys of having additional units on the battlefield for Colquitt would not last.[136]

Shortly after crossing by the southern end of the East Woods, McRae's North Carolinians came in sight of a large enemy force. It was Tyndale's brigade, made up of Ohio regiments and one Pennsylvania regiment. The brigade opened fire as soon as they were able. McRae's North Carolinians replied with their own deadly volleys. Confusion quickly set in with McRae. "Unaccountably to me, an order was given to cease firing," McRae recorded. For some reason, it was thought that General Ripley's brigade was still in action and that the North Carolina Brigade led by McRae were firing into it. Experiencing "great confusion," and facing an enemy not only to the front but also on the right, much of the North Carolina brigade panicked and scattered.[137]

Back in the cornfield, the fighting grew intense. Neither side was willing to quit until the day was won—but this would not be the case. Both sides suffered greatly during the confrontation; the heat of the day led to great fatigue on both sides. The smoke-filled air, along with the stench of death and the cries of the wounded, made matters worse for Union and Confederate alike. The 6th and 27th Georgia, showing no signs of slowing down, continued and, unbelievable to the 27th Indiana, fired a "terrible destructive" fire into both the 3rd Wisconsin and the 27th Indiana. To Colonel Colgrove, it seemed "that our little force would be entirely annihilated."[138]

Prior to setting up their line of defense, the 3rd Wisconsin had been hit hard as they marched toward the cornfield. Unable to fire toward Colquitt's brigade due to the Pennsylvania regiments retreating, several of the men of the 3rd Wisconsin were picked off. Once the field was clear of other Union soldiers, the Wisconsin boys returned fire "with steadiness and spirit," said the colonel of the 3rd Wisconsin, Thomas H. Ruger. After one of the volleys was fired by the 3rd, the 27th Georgia took advantage and moved to within "100 yards" of the Union line but was unable to hold their position. The 2nd Massachusetts fired from their location, causing the 27th Georgia to fall back to their original line. After reloading his musket, Private William T. Leonard from Company C fired off a quick shot at the 27th Georgia men as they fell back. Before Leonard was able to kneel and reload, a Confederate bullet struck him in the chest, just above the heart, knocking him to the ground.

Leonard, believe it or not, survived the serious wound that cracked his fifth rib and left him "quite lame from its affects."[139]

Time seemed to drag, but the heated exchange of musket fire between Colquitt and Gordon's brigade raged on for what felt like "two hours." The Union front, which consisted of the 2nd Massachusetts, the 3rd Wisconsin and the 27th Indiana, fought until "the ammunition in the boxes became nearly exhausted." To the left of the 27th Indiana, the East Woods had been alive with action. Not only had the 10th Maine pushed the 5th Texas, 21st Georgia and the 4th Alabama out of the East Woods, but they, along with Tyndale's brigade, also drew near the cornfield. Finding himself about to be flanked, Colquitt ordered his brigade to abandon the position. "At this time an advance was ordered, and being executed with bayonets," wrote Ruger.[140]

The bayonet charge did not last long. As the 3rd Wisconsin and 27th Indiana advanced through the cornfield, attempting the impossible task of not stepping on the dead and wounded, their advance was ordered to a halt. Off to the east, just south of the East Woods, the Union's Second Corps, under Sumner, was seen marching onto the field. Now halted, both the Wisconsin and Indiana men remained in position as Sumner's front lines moved across their front, marching toward Jackson's left in the West Woods. Though their job was done, all was not quiet. Artillery was still very much active, exploding all around the cornfield and growing more intense with the Second Corps entering the fight.

With the men of the Second Corps now spreading out into lines of battle and taking fire from Jackson's line of defense, the 3rd Wisconsin, along with the rest of Gordon's brigade, left the cornfield. Moving to the East Woods, the Wisconsin regiment was the first to arrive in place, assisting Cothan's Battery, who were helping with the retreat of the rest of Gordon's brigade. For the rest of the day, the 3rd Wisconsin and the rest of the brigade remained in place. Here, they were able to replenish their ammunition, eat and get a little rest. As the battle raged on against Jackson's line, Confederate artillery shells still exploded around the Wisconsin men and the others but caused little damage.[141]

In the East Woods, Colonel Ruger tallied up the total loss for the day. At the start of the battle, the 3rd Wisconsin totaled 340 men, including officers. The loss during the brave yet bloody fight in Miller's Cornfield cost the regiment 198 men. The majority of the 3rd's officers were either killed or wounded to the point where they were unable to return to fight. A total of only four officers remained uninjured. The bravery shown by the men of the 3rd Wisconsin was an unbelievable sight, considering the size and horrible

Where Sumner's corps charged at Antietam. *Library of Congress.*

position they were in during battle. Recalling all the killed and wounded, Ruger said, "It has been impossible in many cases to ascertain the character of the wounds," due the high amount of causalities.[142]

Gordon's brigade "slept upon the bloody field" where they were victorious. Skirmishing here and there between a few regiments and the Confederates continued. For the most part, the men in the East Woods were harassed by Confederate artillery shells exploding, sending dirt and tree branches on the men. On the performance of his brigade, Gordon wrote: "I cannot too highly praise the conduct of my brigade of regiments. I was not disappointed."

It was around 8:40 a.m., and the raging battle had been in progress since daylight. Miller's Cornfield, the plot of land once filled with thick green stalks of corn, was now the scene of complete horror. Filled with the dead

Burying the dead on the battlefield of Antietam. *Library of Congress.*

A Confederate soldier, who, after being wounded, had dragged himself to a little ravine on the hillside, where he died. *Library of Congress.*

and wounded, the screams of the latter could not even be heard by Gordon's men, who now held tight in the East Woods. The air smelled like sulfur, and the artillery fight continued sending shells over to the West Woods, where Stonewall Jackson still held. However, the cornfield and East Woods were now in the hands of the Union. On the other side of the field, only Hood's, Ewell's and Jackson's divisions held the entire Confederate left flank and were tangling with a new corps that had just arrived.

Although the First and Twelfth Corps had gained the hard-fought ground, they suffered heavily for it. Captain Julian Hinkley of Company E, 3rd Wisconsin, noted, "the bodies of brave men were so thickly strewn

Gathered together for burial after the Battle of Antietam. *Library of Congress.*

over it, that one might for rods have walked on corpses without touching the ground." Hooker recalled, "Every stalk of corn in the northern and greater part of the field was cut as closely as could have been done with a knife, and the slain lay in rows precisely as they had stood in their ranks a few moments before." To further describe the scene, Hooker wrote, "It was never my fortune to witness a bloodier, dismal battlefield."[143]

Sharpsburg, Maryland, the small sleepy town that many of the soldiers from Wisconsin had never heard of, was now ingrained in their minds. Blood had been spilled on the fields that would be given the name of the small, rust-colored creek that flowed slowly, undisturbed by time, and that would now be a haunting name that would cause nightmares in the minds of the men from Wisconsin for the rest of their lives.

AFTERWORD

The vicious fighting that the Iron Brigade, along with the 3rd Wisconsin and the rest of the First and Twelfth Corps, took part in is just a portion of the story. Although Wisconsin and the others mentioned were done with the fight, the Battle of Antietam was not yet finished. General Hooker's First Corps and the Confederate left, under Jackson, virtually destroyed each other in the bloody fight on the morning of September 17, 1862. The men on the northern part of the battlefield remained in place, firing shots at one another off and on for the remainder of the day. No formal engagement took place north of town the rest of the day. The bloody battle was far from over, however; it just moved to the south.

The next part took place in the center of Lee's battle line, where his "Old War Horse," General James Longstreet, commanded. Longstreet and his men defended a place that became known as Bloody Lane, or the Sunken Road. Longstreet's troopers would battle it out against elements of General Sumner's Second Corps in what also turned out to be a horrific fight. The bloodshed still does not end here.

Even farther to the south stood a simple bridge used by townspeople to cross Antietam Creek. However, on September 17, the bridge would obtain the name by which it would forever be known: Burnside Bridge. By noon on the seventeenth, General Burnside, along with his Ninth Corps, battled it out with the Confederate right flank. Burnside's Corps exchanged fire with the Confederate divisions under Kemper, Drayton and Jennings. When Burnside was able to finally cross the bridge, the collapsing Confederate line began pulling back. It looked as though Lee's army would be crushed; however, it was not meant to be. A.P. Hill's Corps arrived and saved Lee from what may have been complete destruction. The bloody fight would continue, and the war would not end here as McClellan had hoped.

General McClellan had every intention of renewing the attack on the morning of September 18. Lee was in bad shape, and McClellan knew it. "Our troops were much exhausted and greatly reduced in numbers by fatigue and the casualties of battle. Under these circumstances it was deemed injudicious to push our advantage further in the face of fresh troops of the enemy, much exceeding the number of our own," wrote General Lee. Although by morning on the eighteenth, Lee's army had been strengthened by the arrival of six thousand new troops, another heavy fight just would not happen. The troops were exhausted and hungry, and unlike the Union Army, Lee was not able to replace the men who had been killed, wounded or ran off.[144]

Lee's men remained in place on the eighteenth, and the day passed "without any demonstration" from McClellan's men. This gave Lee the idea that McClellan was waiting on help to arrive before renewing the attack. Lee reported: "As we could not look for a material increase in strength, and the enemy's force could be largely and rapidly augmented, it was not thought prudent to wait until he should be ready again to offer battle. During the night of the 18th the army was accordingly withdrawn to the south side of the Potomac, crossing near Shepherdstown, without loss or molestation."[145]

On the morning of September 19, McClellan sent a reconnaissance across the river that "resulted in ascertaining the near presence of the enemy in some force and in our capturing six guns. A second reconnaissance, the next morning, which, with the first, was made by a small detachment from Porter's corps, resulted in observing a heavy force of the enemy there. The detachment withdrew with slight loss," wrote McClellan.[146]

The pursuit of Lee's army across the Potomac by the Union's Fifth Corps did not get the results McClellan wanted. McClellan's men were pushed back after tangling with Lee's entrenched men at Shepherdstown, resulting in a Confederate victory. The fighting at Shepherdstown marked the end of Lee's Maryland Campaign, and with that, Lee was able to move into the safety of his known lands. McClellan had once again proven himself to be a do-nothing general. Happy for what was perceived as a Union victory, President Lincoln was able to issue his famous Emancipation Proclamation that gave freedom to people held in slavery in the South.

Though Lincoln was happy to issue his proclamation, he once again became irritated with George McClellan's lack of movement. By November of the same year, Lincoln had finally had enough of his commanding general. On November 7, 1862, Major General George B. McClellan was relieved of command for the final time.

With McClellan gone, Lincoln appointed his new choice to lead the Army of the Potomac, and it was none other than Major General Ambrose Burnside. Burnside, who was not capable of leading the entire Army of the Potomac, would show just what a horrible choice Lincoln had made on December 11, 1862, at a town called Fredericksburg.

Following Burnside's blunder at Fredericksburg, a new change in command came in early 1863. This time, Lincoln named the First Corps commander, Major General Joseph Hooker, to lead the Army of the Potomac. Although Hooker's corps fought bravely at Antietam, his lack of leadership showed by May 1863 at the Battle of Chancellorsville. Hooker ignored reports of Confederate movements, and his army was caught off guard, resulting in heavy losses. Hooker, though, was not to lead much longer. By the end of June 1863, Lincoln had removed Hooker from command and promoted Major General George Gordon Meade.

"The grand review at Washington, May 23, 1865. The glorious Army of the Potomac passes the head stand." *Library of Congress.*

Meade had not been in command long before he faced off against Lee at Gettysburg for three intense days of fighting. Gettysburg was a major victory for the Union army; some historians see it as the turning point in the Civil War. Although Meade failed to pursue Lee's badly damaged army when the slow-moving Confederates crossed the Potomac, he did not have much of a choice. Although Lincoln was furious, Meade made the right call. His army was exhausted, and a fast pursuit into another potential engagement may have cost the Army of the Potomac dearly.

Although irritated with Meade, Lincoln allowed him to remain in command. That would not change for the remainder of the war. However, by March 1864, Lincoln decided to promote Ulysses S. Grant to lieutenant general, giving command of the entire Union army to him. Although Grant had done his fighting in the West, he decided to attach his headquarters to the Army of the Potomac. Along with Meade, Grant continued to pursue Lee's army until April 9, 1865, when Lee surrendered his army to Grant. The war was finally over.

Appendix

Antietam Order of Battle

Army of the Potomac

GENERAL HEADQUARTERS
Maj. Gen. George B. McClellan

First Army Corps
Maj. Gen. Joseph Hooker

First Division
Brig. Gen. Rufus King
Brig. Gen. John P. Hatch
Brig. Gen. Abner Doubleday

First Brigade
Colonel Walter Phelps Jr.
22nd New York
24th New York
30th New York
84th New York
2nd U.S. Sharpshooters

Second Brigade
Brig. Gen. Abner Doubleday
7th Indiana
76th New York
95th New York
56th Pennsylvania

Third Brigade
Brig. Gen. Marsena R. Patrick
21st New York
23rd New York
35th New York
80th New York (20th Militia)

Fourth Brigade
Brig. Gen. John Gibbon
19th Indiana
2nd Wisconsin
6th Wisconsin
7th Wisconsin

Artillery
Capt. J. Albert Monroe
New Hampshire Light, 1st Battery
1st Rhode Island Light, Battery D
1st New York Light, Battery L
4th United States, Battery B
Capt. Joseph B. Campbell
Lieut. James Stewart

Second Division
Brig. Gen. James B. Ricketts
First Brigade
Brig. Gen. Abram Duryee
97th New York
104th New York
105th New York
107th Pennsylvania

Second Brigade
Col. William A. Christian
26th New York
26th New York
94th New York
88th Pennsylvania
90th Pennsylvania

Third Brigade
Brig. Gen. George L. Hartsuff
16th Maine
12th Massachusetts
13th Massachusetts
83rd New York (9th Militia)
11th Pennsylvania

Artillery
1st Pennsylvania Light, Battery F
Pennsylvania Light, Battery C

Third Division
Brig. Gen. George G. Meade
First Brigade
Brig. Gen. Truman Seymour
1st Pennsylvania Reserves
2nd Pennsylvania Reserves
5th Pennsylvania Reserves
6th Pennsylvania Reserves
13th Pennsylvania Reserves (1st Rifles)

Second Brigade
Col. Albert Magilton
3rd Pennsylvania Reserves
4th Pennsylvania Reserves
7th Pennsylvania Reserves
8th Pennsylvania Reserves

Third Brigade
Col. Thomas F. Gallagher
9th Pennsylvania Reserves
10th Pennsylvania Reserves
11th Pennsylvania Reserves
12th Pennsylvania Reserves

Artillery
1st Pennsylvania Light, Battery A
1st Pennsylvania Light, Battery B
1st Pennsylvania Light, Battery G
5th United States, Battery C

Sixth Army Corps
Maj. Gen. William B. Franklin

First Division
Maj. Gen. Henry W. Slocum

First Brigade
Col. Alfred T. A. Torbert
1st New Jersey
2nd New Jersey
3rd New Jersey
4th New Jersey

Second Brigade
Col. Joseph J. Bartlett
5th Maine
16th New York
27th New York
96th Pennsylvania
121st New York

Third Brigade
Brig. Gen. John Newton
18th New York
31st New York
32rd New York
96th Pennsylvania

Artillery
Maryland Light, Battery A
Massachusetts Light, Battery A
New Jersey Light, Battery A
2nd United States, Battery D

Second Division
Maj. Gen. William F. Smith

First Brigade
Brig. Gen. Winfield S. Hancock
6th Maine
43rd New York
49th Pennsylvania
137th Pennsylvania
5th Wisconsin

Second Brigade
Brig. Gen. W.T.H. Brooks
2nd Vermont
3rd Vermont
4th Vermont
5th Vermont
6th Vermont

Third Brigade
Col. William H. Irwin
7th Maine
20th New York
33rd New York
49th New York
77th New York

Artillery
Maryland Light, Battery B
New York Light, 1st Battery
5th United States, Battery F

Twelfth Army Corps
Maj. Gen. Joseph K.F. Mansfield
Brig. Gen. Alpheus, S. Williams

First Division
Brig. Gen. Alpheus S. Williams

First Brigade
Brig. Gen. Samuel W. Crawford
5th Connecticut
10th Maine
28th New York
46th Pennsylvania
124th Pennsylvania
125th Pennsylvania
128th Pennsylvania

Third Brigade
Brig. Gen. George H. Gordon
27th Indiana
2nd Massachusetts
13th New Jersey
107th New York
3rd Wisconsin
Zouaves d'Afrique, Pennsylvania

Second Division
Brig. Gen, George S. Green

First Brigade
Lt. Col. Hector Tyndale
5th Ohio
7th Ohio
29th Ohio
66th Ohio
28th Pennsylvania

Second Brigade
Col. Henry J. Stainrook
3rd Maryland
102nd New York
109th Pennsylvania
111th Pennsylvania

Third Brigade
Col. William B. Goodrich
3rd Delaware
Purnell Legion Maryland
60th New York
78th New York

Artillery
Maine Light, 4th Battery
Maine Light, 6th Battery
1st New York Light, Battery M
New York Light, 10th Battery
Pennsylvania Light, Battery E
Pennsylvania Light, Battery F
4th United States, Battery F

Cavalry Division
Brig. Gen. Alfred Pleasonton

First Brigade
Maj. Charles J. Whiting
5th United States
6th United States

Second Brigade
Col. John F. Farnsworth
8th Illinois
3rd Indiana

1st Massachusetts
8th Pennsylvania

Third Brigade
Col. Richard H. Rush
4th Pennsylvania
6th Pennsylvania

Fourth Brigade
Col. Andrew T. McReynolds
1st New York
12th Pennsylvania

Fifth Brigade
Col. Benjamin F. Davis
8th New York
3rd Pennsylvania

Artillery
2nd United States, Battery A
2nd United States, Batteries B and L
2nd United States, Battery M
3rd United States, Batteries C and G

Unattached
1st Maine Cavalry
15th Pennsylvania Cavalry
(detachment)

CONFEDERATE ORDER OF BATTLE

General Robert E. Lee, Commanding

Longstreet's Command
Maj. Gen. James Longstreet

McLaws's Division
Maj. Gen. Lafayette McLaws

Cobb's Brigade
Cobb's (Georgia) Legion
16th Georgia
24th Georgia
15th North Carolina

Semmes's Brigade
Brig. Gen. Paul J. Semmes
10th Georgia
53rd Georgia
15th Virginia
32nd Virginia

Artillery
Manly's (North Carolina) Battery
Pulaski (Georgia) Artillery
Richmond (Fayette) Artillery
Richmond Howitzers (1st Company)
Troup (Georgia) Artillery

Anderson's Division
Maj. Gen. Richard H. Anderson

Mahone's Brigade
Col. William A. Parham
6th Virginia
12th Virginia
16th Virginia

41st Virginia
61st Virginia

Jones's Division
Brig. Gen. David R. Jones

Toombs's Brigade
Brig. Gen. Robert Toombs
2nd Georgia
15th Georgia
17th Georgia
20th Georgia

Drayton's Brigade
Brig. Gen. Thomas F. Drayton
50th Georgia
51st Georgia
15th South Carolina

Pickett's Brigade
Brig. Gen. R.B. Garnett
8th Virginia
18th Virginia
19th Virginia
28th Virginia
56th Virginia

Kemper's Brigade
Brig. Gen. J.L. Kemper
1st Virginia
7th Virginia
11th Virginia
17th Virginia
24th Virginia

Jenkins's Brigade
Col. Joseph Walker
1st South Carolina (Volunteers)
2nd South Carolina Rifles

5th South Carolina
6th South Carolina
4th South Carolina Battalion
Palmetto (SouthCarolina)
    Sharpshooters

Anderson's Brigade
Col. George T. Anderson
1st Georgia (Regulars)
7th Georgia
8th Georgia
9th Georgia
11th Georgia

Hood's Division
Brig. Gen. John B. Hood

Hood's Brigade
Col. W.T. Wofford
18th Georgia
Hampton (South Carolina) Legion
1st Texas
4th Texas
5th Texas

Law's Brigade
Col. E.M. Law
4th Alabama
2nd Mississippi
11th Mississippi
6th North Carolina

Evans's Brigade
Brig. Gen. Nathan Evans
Holcombe (South Carolina) Legion
Macbeth (South Carolina) Artillery
17th South Carolina
18th South Carolina
22nd South Carolina
23rd South Carolina

Lee's Battalion
Col. S.D. Lee
Ashland (Virginia) Artillery
Bedford (Virginia) Artillery

Brooks (South Carolina) Artillery
Eubank's (Virginia) Battery
Madison (Louisiana) Light Artillery
Parker's (Virginia) Battery

Jackson's Command
Maj. Gen. Thomas J. Jackson

Ewell's Division
Brig. Gen. A.R. Lawton

Lawton's Brigade
Col. M. Douglass
13th Georgia
26th Georgia
31st Georgia
38th Georgia
60th Georgia
61st Georgia

Early's Brigade
Brig. Gen. Jubal Early
Col. William Smith
13th Virginia
25th Virginia
31st Virginia
44th Virginia
49th Virginia
52nd Virginia
58th Virginia

Trimble's Brigade
Col. James A. Walker
15th Alabama
12th Georgia
21st Georgia
21st North Carolina
1st North Carolina Battalion

Hays's Brigade
Brig. Gen. Harry T. Hays
5th Louisiana
6th Louisiana
7th Louisiana
8th Louisiana
14th Louisiana

Jackson's Division
Brig. Gen. John R. Jones
Brig. Gen. W E. Starke
Col. A.J. Grigsby

Winder's Brigade
Col. A.J. GRIGSBY
2nd Virginia
4th Virginia
5th Virginia
27th Virginia
33rd Virginia

Taliaferro's Brigade
47th Alabama
48th Alabama
10th Virginia
23rd Virginia
37th Virginia

Jones's Brigade
Col. B.T. Johnson
21st Virginia
42nd Virginia
48th Virginia
1st Virginia Battalion

Starke's Brigade
Brig. Gen. William E. Starke
Coppens's (Louisiana) Battalion
1st Louisiana
2nd Louisiana
9th Louisiana
10th Louisiana
15th Louisiana

Artillery
Alleghany (Virginia) Artillery
 (Carpenter's Battery)
Brockenbrough's (Maryland) battery
Danville (Virginia) Artillery
 (Wooding's Battery)
Hampden (Virginia) Artillery
 (Caskie's Battery)
Lee (Virginia) Battery (Raine's
 Battery)
Rockbridge (Virginia) Artillery
 (Poague's Battery)

Hill's Division
Maj. Gen. Daniel H. Hill

Ripley's Brigade
Brig. Gen. Roswell S. Ripley
Col. George Doles
4th Georgia
44th Georgia
1st North Carolina
3rd North Carolina

Rodes's Brigade
Brig. Gen. R.E. Rodes
3rd Alabama
5th Alabama
6th Alabama
12th Alabama
26th Alabama

Garland's Brigade
Brig. Gen. Samuel Garland Jr.
Col. D.K. McRae
5th North Carolina
12th North Carolina
13th North Carolina
20th North Carolina
23rd North Carolina

Anderson's Brigade
Brig. Gen. George B. Anderson
2nd North Carolina
4th North Carolina
14th North Carolina
30th North Carolina

Colquitt's Brigade
Col. A.H. Colquitt
13th Alabama
6th Georgia
23d Georgia
27th Georgia
28th Georgia

Cavalry
Maj. Gen. James E.B. Stuart

Hampton's Brigade
Brig. Gen. Wade Hampton
Cobb's (Georgia) Legion
Jefferson Davis Legion
1st North Carolina
2nd South Carolina
10th Virginia

Lee's Brigade
Brig. Gen. Fitzhugh Lee
1st Virginia
3rd Virginia
4th Virginia
5th Virginia
9th Virginia

Robertson's Brigade
Col. Thomas T. Munford
2nd Virginia
6th Virginia
7th Virginia
12th Virginia
17th Virginia Battalion

Horse Artillery
Capt. John Pelham
Chew's (Virginia) Battery
Hart's (South Carolina) battery
Pelham's (Virginia) battery

NOTES

Introduction

1. "Randall's Proclamation," *State Journal* (Madison, WI), April 16, 1861.
2. "Meeting Last Night!," *State Journal*, April 19, 1861.

Chapter 1

3. Ibid., 25–26.
4. George H. Otis, *The Second Wisconsin Infantry*, ed. Alan D. Gaff (Dayton, OH: Morningside Bookshop, 1984), 29.
5. E.B. Quiner, *Military History of Wisconsin* (Chicago: Clarke and Company, 1866).
6. Ibid.
7. Ibid.
8. Quiner, 36; Rufus R. Dawes, *Service with the Sixth Wisconsin* (Marietta, OH: Alderman & Sons, 1890), 19.
9. "Sixth Wisconsin Infantry History," Wisconsin Historical Society, accessed September 14, 2018, www.wisconsinhistory.org/Records/Article/CS2365.
10. Ibid.

Chapter 2

11. U.S. War Department, *War of the Rebellion, A Compilation of the Official Records of the Union and Confederate Armies*, Series 1, vol. 19, part 2, 590 (hereafter cited as *OR*; citations are Series 1 unless otherwise noted).

12. Lee's Report, *OR*, vol. 19, part 1, 145.

13. Lee's Letter to Davis, *OR*, vol. 19, part 2, 596.

14. James L. Coker, *History of Company G Ninth S.C. Regiment Infantry, S.C. Army and of Company E, Sixth S.C. Regiment Infantry C.S. Army* (Greenwood, SC: Attic Press), 103; Robert T. Hubard, Notebook 1860–1866, "Damnation of Vancouver," and "Turvey" Manuscripts, Acc. No. 10522, Manuscript Department, University of Virginia, Charlottesville, Virginia, 14.

15. Stuart's Report, *OR*, vol. 19, part 1, 815.

16. General Orders No. 102, *OR*, vol. 19, part 2, 592.

17. James Longstreet, *From Manassas to Appomattox: Memoirs of the Civil War in America* (Philadelphia: J.B. Lippincott, 1896); Lee's Report, *OR*, vol. 19, part 1, 145.

18. Spencer G. Welch, letter, September 24, 1862.

19. McClellan's Report, *OR*, vol. 19, part 1, 25.

20. Ibid.

21.Burnside's Report, *OR*, vol. 19, part 1. 416.

22. Scott D. Hartwig, *To Antietam Creek: The Maryland Campaign of September 1862* (Baltimore, MD: Johns Hopkins University Press, 2012).

23.McClellan's Report, *OR*, vol. 19, part 1, 26.

24. McClellan to Lincoln, *OR*, vol. 19, part 2, 281.

25. John David Hoptak, *The Battle of South Mountain* (Charleston, SC: The History Press, 2011).

26. Ibid., 35.

Chapter 3

27. Slocum's Report, *OR*, vol. 19, part 1, 380; Hoptak, *Battle of South Mountain*, 136.

28. Ezra A. Carman, *The Maryland Campaign of September 1862*, vol. 1, *South Mountain*, ed. Thomas Clemens, 3 vols. (El Dorado Hills, CA: Savas Beatie, 2010), 301; Stuart's Report, *OR*, vol. 19, part 1, 818.

29. Bartlett's Report, *OR*, vol. 19, part 1, 388; Slocum's Report, *OR*, vol. 19, part 1, 380.

30. Slocum's Report, *OR*, vol. 19, part 1, 380.

31. Cobb's Report, *OR*, vol. 19, part 1, 870.

32. Ibid.

33. Cobb's Report, *OR*, vol. 19, part 1, 870–71.

34. Ibid., 871; Carman, *Maryland Campaign*, 310.

35. D.H. Hill's Report, *OR*, vol. 19, part 1, 1019. Stephen W. Sears, *Landscape Turned Red: The Battle of Antietam* (New York: Mariner Books, 1983), 128.

36. Colquitt's Report, *OR*, vol. 19, part 1, 1052.

37. John M. Priest, *Before Antietam: The Battle of South Mountain* (Shippensburg, PA: White Mane Publishing), 1992, 134; McRae's Report, *OR*, vol. 19, part 1, 1040.

38. McRae's Report, *OR*, vol. 19, part 1, 1040.

39. Priest, *Before Antietam*, 137.

40. Carman, *Maryland Campaign*, 1:317.

41. Cox's Report, *OR*, vol. 19, part 1, 458.

42. Ibid., 458–59; Hoptak, *Battle of South Mountain*, 44; Carman, *Maryland Campaign*, 1:319.

43. Cox's Report, *OR*, vol. 19, part 1, 458; Carman, *Maryland Campaign*, 1:318–19.

44. McRae's Report, *OR*, vol. 19, part 1. 1040.

45. Carman, *Maryland Campaign*, 1:324–25; McRae's Report, *OR*, vol. 19, part 1, 1040; Cox's Report, *OR*, vol. 19, part 1, 459.

46. Hoptak, *Battle of South Mountain*, 49; Carman, *Maryland Campaign*, 1:326; Cox's Report, *OR*, vol. 19, part 1, 459.

47. Carman, *Maryland Campaign*, 1:326; Hoptak, *Battle of South Mountain*, 51; McRae's Report, *OR*, vol. 19, part 1, 1040–41.

48. McRae's Report, *OR*, vol. 1, part 1, 1040; Priest, *Before Antietam*, 149–50.

49. McRae's Report, 1040–41.

50. Carman, *Maryland Campaign*, 1:327.

51. Cox's Report, *OR*, vol. 19, part 1, 459; Carman, *Maryland Campaign*, 1:332.

52. Hill's Report, *OR*, vol. 19, part 1, 1019-20.

53. Cox's Report, *OR*, vol. 19, part 1, 460; D.H. Hill's Report, *OR*, part 1, 1020.

54. D.H. Hill's Report, *OR*, part 1, 1021–22.

55. Carman, *Maryland Campaign*.

56. Hooker's Report, *OR*, vol. 19, part 1, 214.

57. Ibid

58. Carman, *Maryland Campaign*, 1:349.

59. Hoptak, *Battle of South Mountain*, 99.

60. Rodes's Report, *OR*, vol. 19, part 1, 1035.

61. Ibid

62. Seymour's Report, *OR*, vol. 19, part 1, 272.

63. Hartwig, *To Antietam Creek*, 388.

64. Rodes's, *OR*, vol. 19, part 1, 1035.

65. Anderson's Report, *OR*, vol. 19, part 1, 275.

66. Magilton's Report, *OR*, vol. 19, part 1, 273.

67. Evans's Report, *OR*, vol. 19, part 1, 939.

68. Carman, *Maryland Campaign*, 1:355.

69. Wallace's Report, *OR*, vol. 19, part 1, 947.

70. Carman, *Maryland Campaign*, 1:356.

71. Hatch's Report, *OR*, vol. 19, part 1, 220–21.

72. Priest, *Before Antietam*.

73. Garnett's Report, *OR*, vol. 19, part 1, 894.

74. Patrick's Report, *OR*, vol. 19, part 1, 242.

75. Carman, *Maryland Campaign*, 1:360–61.

76. A.F. Lee letter, September 30, 1862.

77. John Gibbon, *At Gettysburg and Elsewhere: The Civil War Memoir of John Gibbon* (Bellevue, WA: Big Byte Books, 2016); Carman, *Maryland Campaign*, 1:365.

78. Fairchild's Report, *OR*, vol. 19, part 1, 252–53.

79. Callis's Report, *OR*, vol. 19, part 1, 256–57.

80. Priest, *Before Antietam*, 268.

81. Hoptak, *Battle of South Mountain*, 129; Priest, *Before Antietam*, 269; Bregg's Report, *OR*, vol. 19, part 1, 253–54; William P. Taylor letter, September 18, 1862.

82. *State Journal*, September 16, 1862.

Chapter 4

83. Otis, *Second Wisconsin Infantry*, 258–59.

84. McClellan's Report, *OR*, vol. 19, part 1, 26–27.

85. Gibbon, *At Gettysburg*, 64.

86. Carman, *Maryland Campaign*, 1:411.

87. McClellan's Report, *OR*, vol. 19, part 1, 27.

88. Hooker's Report, *OR*, vol. 19, part 1, 217.

Chapter 5

89. Jackson's Report, *OR*, vol. 19, part 1, 955.

90. Carman, *Maryland Campaign*, 2:53.

91. Otis, *Second Wisconsin Infantry*, 260.

92. Doubleday's Report, *OR*, vol. 19, part 1, 223–24; John M. Priest, *Antietam: The Soldiers Battle* (New York: Oxford University Press, 1989), 31.

93. Priest, *Antietam*, 3; Otis, *Second Wisconsin Infantry*, 261.

94. Dawes, *Service with the Sixth Wisconsin*, 88.

95. Carman, *Maryland Campaign*, vol. 2, *Antietam*, 71.

96. Gibbon, *At Gettysburg*, 65–66.

97. Phelps's Report, *OR*, vol. 19, part 1, 233. Carman, *Maryland Campaign*, 2:73.

98. Cullen B. Aubery, *Echoes from the Marches of the Famous Iron Brigade: Unwritten Stories of That Famous Organization* (Milwaukee, Wisconsin, 1902).

99. Jackson's Report, *OR*, vol. 19, part 1, 956; General Early's Report, *OR* vol. 19, part 1, 967–68.

100. Ricketts' Report, *OR*, vol. 19, part 1, 259; Carman, *Maryland Campaign*, 2:58–59.

101. Walker's Report, OR, vol. 19, part 1, 976–77.

102. Hays's Report, *OR*, vol. 19, part 1, 978.

103. Bragg's Report. *OR*, vol. 19, part 1, 255.

104. Dawes, *Service with the Sixth Wisconsin*, 89.

105. Ibid, 89–90.

106. Elon Brown, letter to his brothers and sisters, September 19, 1862; Otis, *Second Wisconsin Infantry*, 261, 324.

107. Charles Delany, undated letter home.

108. J.R. Jones's Report, *OR*, vol. 19, part 1, 1008.

109. Callis's Report, *OR*, vol. 19, part 1, 258.

110. Dawes, *Service with the Sixth Wisconsin*, 91.

111. Carman, *Maryland Campaign*, 2:78; Dawes, *Service with the Sixth Wisconsin*, 91.

112. Phelps's Report, *OR*, vol. 19, part 1, 233. Carman, *Maryland Campaign*, 2:78.

113. Spencer G. Welch, letter home, dated September 24, 1862.

114. William P. Taylor, undated letter to his father.

115. J.B. David, letter to Mr. Taplin, September 24, 1862.

116. Dudley's Report, *OR*, vol. 19, part 1, 251.

117. Lyle's Report, *OR*, vol. 19, part 1, 266.

118. Carman, *Maryland Campaign*, 2:81; Phelps's Report, *OR*, vol. 19, part 1, 233.

119. Hood's Report, *OR*, vol. 19, part 1, 923.

120. Ibid; Priest, *Antietam*, 55.

121. Dawes, *Service with the Sixth Wisconsin*, 92; Wofford's Report, *OR*, vol. 19, part 1, 928.

122. Lyle's Report, *OR*, vol. 19, part 1, 266.

123. Law's Report, *OR*, vol. 19, part 1, 938.

124. Ibid.

125. Wofford's Report. *OR*, vol. 19, part 1, 928.

126. Ibid.

127. Ripley's Report, *OR*, vol. 19, part 1, 1033; Bradley M. Gottfried, *The Maps of Antietam* (El Dorado Hills, CA: Savas Beatie, 2012).

128. Callis Report, *OR*, vol. 19, part 1, 258; Carman, *Maryland Campaign*, 1:107.

129. William T. Leonard, letter to his cousin, December 31, 1863.

130. Gordon's Report, *OR*, vol. 19, part 1, 495.

131. Crawford's Report, *OR*, vol. 19, part 1, 484–85.

132. Wanner's Report, *OR*, vol. 19, part 1, 493.

133. Gordon's Report, *OR*, vol. 19, part 1, 495.

134. Alfred Siegel, *William Roberts: His Life, Military Career and Legacy* (California, 2000). Siegel is the great-grandson of William Roberts.

135. Colgrove's Report, *OR*, vol. 19, part 1, 498.

136. McRae's Report, *OR*, vol. 19, part 1, 1043.

137. Ibid.

138. Colgrove's Report, *OR*, vol. 19, part 1, 499.

139. Leonard, letter to his cousin; Ruger's Report, *OR*, vol. 19, part 1, 503.

140. Ruger's Report, *OR*, vol. 19, part 1, 503. Colgrove's Report, *OR*, vol. 19, part 1, 499.

141. Ruger's Report, *OR*, vol. 19, part 1, 504.

142. Ibid.

143. Siegel, *William Roberts*; Hooker's Report, *OR*, vol. 19, part 1, 218.

Afterword

144. Lee's Report. *OR*, vol. 19, part 1, 151.

145. Ibid.

146. McClellan's Report, *OR*, vol. 19, part 1, 32.

INDEX

About the Author

C al Schoonover is the author of several articles relating to the Civil War and true crimes. After earning his BA in eighteenth- and nineteenth-century military history, he went on to earn his MA in history, concentrating on the Civil War. He is currently pursuing his PhD in American history. Cal currently resides in Janesville, Wisconsin, with his son, James.